Bulletp

How to Make Yourself Indispensable

Bulletproof

How to Make Yourself Indispensable

Mark C. Scott

ARROW

Published by Arrow in 2002

1 3 5 7 9 10 8 6 4 2

First published by Arrow in 2002.

Arrow
The Random House Group Limited
20 Vauxhall Bridge Road, London SW1V 2SA

Random House Australia (Pty) Limited
20 Alfred Street, Milsons Point, Sydney,
New South Wales 2061, Australia

Random House New Zealand Limited
18 Poland Road, Glenfield,
Auckland 10, New Zealand

Random House South Africa (Pty) Limited
Endulini, 5a Jubilee Road, Parktown 2193, South Africa

The Random House Group Limited Reg. No. 954009

www.randomhouse.co.uk

A CIP catalogue record for this book
is available from the British Library

Papers used by Random House UK Limited are natural, recyclable products made from wood grown in sustainable forests. The manufacturing processes conform to the environmental regulations of the country of origin.

ISBN 0 7126 2493 7

Typeset by MATS, Southend-on-Sea, Essex
Printed and bound in the United Kingdom by
Bookmarque, Croydon, Surrey

For Zac Woolfitt

'IL importante d'essere umano . . .'
Leonardo Bruni, Florence, 1431

Author's Note

This book has only been possible as a result of a huge amount of other people's wisdom. Particular thanks are due to the many friends and colleagues who have generously furnished me with their insights over the years. As one of them warned me when I mentioned the plan to write this book, *'It may be that your sole purpose in life is simply to serve as a warning to others.'* Finally, I owe a debt of gratitude to the editorial acumen of Clare Smith and Tiffany Stansfield.

Contents:

INTRODUCTION

'Experience is something you don't get until just after you need it.'

The threat of redundancy and under employment are a source of immense psychological strain to many of us, whether we work for a large firm or, as many of us now do, as freelance consultants. All too often it feels like our employer holds all the cards. It need not be that way. This book is intended to redress the balance.

Its foundation stone is a simple observation – that the strategic tools firms use to improve their competitiveness can readily be used by us to protect our own positions. The business 'gurus' always talk about the competitive advantage of the firm. It is time we started talking about the competitive advantage of the individual. There is no reason we cannot borrow the tools developed by firms for our own advantage. Now is the time to level the playing field while you have an opportunity to do so.

As a working adult who has gone through the experience of redundancy, there is a persistent image that haunts me. The forty-five year old man or woman, sitting rigidly at her desk, a pink slip laid out on the table in front of her. She has the dazed, shell-shocked look of someone who has just seen their world evaporate before them – a haunted, hollowed-out vacancy. Everyone in the office has probably sensed something is about to happen. The tension in the awkward silences has been palpable. Then, one afternoon, she is called aside into a room and the door is closed behind her. Bang.

For the firm collectively there is a price to be paid. There always is for witnessing the fall of a colleague. No one escapes with a clear conscience. The relief of those left behind is tainted with guilt. We share a collective sense of responsibility. Then the lingering fear begins to gather that next it will be you.

For me it is a very personal memory. As a ten-year-old child, I can recall my grandfather returning like a man defeated from battle. Stunned, and exhausted. I didn't really understand what had happened at the time. But I was old enough to clearly see the change it brought about in him. I vowed then to never let the same humiliation happen to me, to somehow be smarter. Then, bingo. Twenty years later, out of a clear blue sky it did. I was thirty, and at that stage of life when dreams are easily shattered. I never imagined that fate would befall me. The feeling of powerlessness and anger is one I have never experienced so intensely before or since.

If the fault can be laid at one's own feet, it would be one thing. If you have screwed up badly, been abusive to colleagues, made illicit use of the company internet, you would have to accept the punishment. But so often it happens through no fault of one's own. Perhaps the company has over-borrowed from the banks to buy up other companies. Perhaps it has misled its investors about its potential. Perhaps it is just down to plain mismanagement from the top. When firms decide to get rid of staff or freelance consultants, it is usually for reasons nothing to do with the individuals concerned. In the downsizing game, we become just numbers on a financial statement. That is what makes it such a frightening and humiliating experience. It is also intensely unpredictable.

If you are anything like me, you continually have to remind yourself that good judgement comes from bad experience and a lot of that comes from bad judgement. This book shows that there are some simple approaches you can adopt to secure yourself in your place of employment by making better judgements. Once you are secure, then it is up to you to thrive and expand. To do so you need to borrow from the armoury of business strategy; to think of yourself the same way companies do.

The great thing is, this will not be achieved at the cost of your employer. Quite the reverse. Any company is no better than the people of which it is comprised. A firm comprised of a population of highly competitive individuals is likely to be more competitive collectively. It is win win. And it is also hugely rewarding.

Step 1: Differentiate or Die

Once all the razz matazz is stripped away, there are only two strategies available to a firm. Either it can choose to compete based on price or it can choose to compete based on some form of differentiation. Corporate strategy has at its heart a simple choice – whether to pursue a low cost strategy or command a premium. Either strategy can result in a profitable position, but they imply fundamentally different objectives and demand very different skills.

In order to compete on price, a firm has to be low cost. All frills have to be sacrificed in the interests of delivering the lowest price product available. The preoccupation of management is efficiency. It is inevitably a very inward focusing mentality, comprised of honing down internal processes, reducing supply costs and minimising labour. By contrast, the objective of differentiation is to command a higher price. This is an intensely outward facing strategy. There is far less concern for efficiency and unit cost. To differentiate its products, the firm has to focus its energies on branding, high quality standards, outstanding customer service and superior technology. That means heavy investment, often in creativity and talent.

At its core, strategy is no more complicated than a choice as to which of these paths to take. It is virtually impossible to combine the two. The products of the world can be divided into two camps – Coke versus Cola Aid, Saks versus Marks & Spencer, Asprey versus Ratners, Rolls versus Mondeo. We live in a two-track world.

ONE SIMPLE CHOICE:

So what is the relevance of this? We are not used to thinking of ourselves as a business. We do not measure the value of our personal equity, we do not consider how to advance the progress of our personal brand. But if you think about it that is a curious thing. All we have is our time, our skill and our reputation. The question is how do we best sell them and how do we defend their value in the eyes of our employer?

You need to start by thinking about your own positioning in a strategic manner. You are a one person company competing with rival individuals for a stable position with your one customer. Like any company, you have to pick your strategy. Like a firm, you have one fundamental strategic choice – to be low cost or to be differentiated. This is the crux of all career decisions, the universal fork in the road. Head down one path and your aim is to keep your head firmly below the parapet and conform to job descriptions. As long as you are not too costly and place few demands on the firm or client, you will have dug your trench and can defend yourself. Take the other route and you are fully exposed as something different. You are costly and demanding, and you are adamant that your contribution is unique.

The low cost route is always the path of least resistance. It is relatively simple. Saddled with heavy burdens of responsibility – mortgage, school fees, babies on the way – by default we often take the first path. All too often it is assumed that the low cost route is the only secure, rational decision, particularly in harder economic times. Career progression is slow, steady and unexceptional and therefore, it would be assumed, more secure.

Be prepared. This book argues forcibly that this is a bad strategy.

BUILT TO LAST

Differentiation has shown itself to be the more sustainable strategy of the two. The average large firm only survives for thirty-eight years, marginally less than the average human career. But those firms that have differentiated themselves tend to be the enduring stars of our corporate galaxy. Virtually every firm whose name you can readily recall – from Coke to Disney to Shell – will be differentiated, charging a premium for outstanding products and services. Those who compete on cost solely, continually find themselves under attack from lower cost players and contracting margins. The low cost strategy is one of diminishing spirals. It is seductively easy to get drawn in but it leads inexorably to oblivion.

Differentiation is a far better path to job security. It holds the potential for better rewards and greater recognition. But it is not a strategy many people consciously lay out for themselves. Nor is it an easy strategy to accomplish. It requires ingenuity, inventiveness, flexibility and courage – qualities few of us have in abundance, particularly when we are hovering in perpetual overdraft. But embracing a strategy of differentiation can be wonderfully enervating. It provides clarity about the work you do and gives you clear goals to aim for.

There are twenty-eight steps to a successful personal differentiation strategy. Mastery of the first fifteen will help you secure your position. The next thirteen are embellishments on the basic strategy, enabling you to thrive and prosper. That's where we go next.

The takeaway

It is important that the ideas in this book are succinct, practical and can quickly be put to use. So at the end of each section, I will summarise the core idea in two or three sentences. The key to Step 1 is as follows:

> The heart of a robust personal strategy is the concept of differentiation. Unless you can succeed in differentiating yourself adequately from those around you, you will not survive any purging or downsizing that your employer or client decides to embark on. The equation is a simple one: **differentiate or die**.

A TALE OF TWO DISMISSALS

If you are under pressure at work, this probably all sounds intensely theoretical. So let me introduce you to three people – Jo Parker, Joan Milroy and John Mowbray – who not long back faced the metaphorical bullet. As usual in these situations, they had no idea why. It just happened. They each emerged from the situation very differently, and their contrasting reactions provide invaluable insights into the practical application of the twenty-eight steps.

The summer of 2000 was, unusually for England, a real summer. For three months the sun transformed the English landscape to a lush green. The vast body of the Thames, visible from the second floor of Communicopia's building, had diminished to a languid flow. There was a general sense around the corporate HQ of well-being. Business always slowed in the summer but, rather than moan, most people seemed to have welcomed the lull as a long deserved break from years of meteoric expansion.

That was almost two months before our story started. How things had changed in two months. As Jo looked back, it was as if there had never been a summer at all. There were three people waiting in the ante-room to John Drinkwater's office suite, sitting in silence. The office was on the fifth floor, with far-reaching views down the river as far as the Houses of Parliament.

John Drinkwater was a formidable figure at the best of times. His father had reputedly worked in a meat packing plant on the shores of the Delaware in Pennsylvania, USA, bloody and hardened, from a line of Irish immigrants. Somehow, not all the blood had been washed out of the Drinkwater genes. Perhaps that was why he instilled such a mixture of admiration and dread. Yet, despite the bullying, for years he had inspired everyone around him with a sense of purpose and energy. He was rewriting the rules and, for all the stress this brought, he had always been loyally followed.

Drinkwater founded Communicopia Group from a basement in Philadelphia's China Town. Its first title was a monthly newspaper for the local food industry. He quickly realised that organic growth was for saints and martyrs. The road to riches was to buy up every good competitor he could talk into selling. That was back in the giddy days of the late-eighties when venture capital money was flowing like manna.

By 1989, he had acquired a small magazine group in London, a real coup for an unknown player from three thousand miles away. He relocated the business to London and in 1990 took it public on the London Stock Exchange. He always told people he would conquer the old country and in some ways he had. Ten years later the man was a legend. He had grown his grubby magazine into a multinational media powerhouse. Spanning every conceivable type of trade publication, Communicopia had become the investment bankers' dream, growing through remorseless acquisition, turning the cosy life-style industry of Soho and Covent Garden into a global cash machine. By the summer of 2000 the firm employed over ten thousand people and was poised to enter the Footsie 100, the ultimate accreditation outside Wall Street.

But despite the outward success and accolades, the

group was beginning to show the strain of a decade of breakneck expansion. The cracks were subtle and easily overlooked by enthusiastic investors. But to the observant insider the signs were there to be read. A few of the businesses had begun to unravel. The debt mountain that had financed the expansion was showing a nagging resistance to diminish in size. It was beginning to become clear that many of the promises that had been made to analysts were going to prove hard to fulfil.

During the summer of 2000 there was an eerie silence from the senior management group. Probably only a handful of people can have even had an inkling that anything was as bad as it actually was. Then suddenly, one morning in September, John Drinkwater announced that he was going to have to reduce costs.

The effect of the news had spread around the organisation like wild-fire. Jo Parker learnt about it when she read the departmental memo on her desk that morning. She had only returned from maternity leave three months before. Tearing herself away from the baby had taken resolve. And now, three months later, every ounce of faith she had placed in herself, in the company, was being tested. She had simply never conceived this could ever happen to her.

She had re-read the memo half a dozen times. Other than the name in the top left corner, it was clearly a form letter. Everyone had got one. Buried amongst twenty lines of verbiage – *due to unforeseen difficulties . . . the severity of the market downturn . . . pressure on margins . . . we all must do our duty to our shareholders* – was a single fact. Thirty per cent of central overhead was going to be removed by December. It was slaughter. One in three people would be out of a job by Christmas. For a brief moment she felt the tears well-up and choke her. Then, with some effort, Jo had managed to regain her composure.

Jo Parker, Joan Milroy and John Mowbray had been sitting outside Drinkwater's office for half an hour, saying nothing to each other. But none of them had any doubt what fate awaited them. The odds were simple. Only one of them would be leaving Drinkwater's office with a job. Oddly, Jo found the fact that she was not alone somehow comforting.

The three made an improbable peer group. They had known each other for about two years. John Mowbray had joined at the about the same time as Jo, as an analyst in the accounting department. Joan Milroy had been there from the very beginning. She had joined as a temp in 1989 and fought her way with honesty and perseverance to the post of deputy office manager. At fifty-one she was a good ten years older than Jo.

John was the hotshot. Jo had no real problem in admitting it to herself. He had been hired as an MBA from London Business School by the director of finance. He was probably no more than thirty, almost ten years younger than her – the blue-eyed boy groomed for glory. It was galling how he could so effortlessly swan under the wing of senior management. But after two years she had to admit she didn't dislike him. They had collaborated on a marketing plan together and she had been impressed by his even handedness towards her. He was the last person she could imagine being fired. It had actually shocked her seeing him enter the lobby and take the seat opposite her. But then she reminded herself, there was absolutely no chance he would get the bullet. The firm was pinning its future on the likes of John Mowbray.

Joan Milroy was very different. She worked in administration on the floor below public relations where Jo worked. All Joan seemed to have in life was her work. She clearly poured her heart and soul into it with an all-consuming passion. Jo was sure it would be a huge blow for her to be fired. She would feel she had failed at life. Jo was pretty certain she was married but that there was something wrong with her husband. Perhaps he was disabled or something like that. She had a silver framed picture of him as a young man in military uniform on her desk.

They sat in brittle silence for almost fifteen minutes. Jo suspected they were all feeling the same thing, and it was that suspicion which inspired her finally to break the silence.

'What I don't understand is that only three months ago we were being told how amazingly the business was performing. They were talking about new stock option packages for employees, a possible pay rise. I don't know about you, but the PR budget was almost doubled in the first half of the year. I've never seen it busier. What on earth happened?' Jo ran her hand through her hair in a gesture of pure irritation.

'It's simple,' John Mowbray responded after a pause. 'We completely overestimated revenues for the year. There's been a slowdown. Clients are cutting advertising budgets.'

For whatever reason, Jo had the impression that he didn't quite believe what he was saying, as if he knew far more of what was happening than he was letting on. That unnerved her.

'Who overestimated? I don't know about you, but isn't that something management's responsible for? Besides, aren't you guys in finance meant to keep a handle on that sort of thing?' she continued.

'I guess.'

He was cautious about being critical. John Mowbray was a straight arrow. Disloyalty did not come to him easily.

'Surely you must have known something was wrong?' Jo continued.

'I know the first half was OK. Earnings were not great but cash flow was on track. There's been no formal profits warning.'

'We're not all finance whizzes John. What does that mean in normal speak?' Jo retorted irritably. 'And they tell us like this?' she continued, tapping the single sheet of paper on her lap.

'It does seem a clumsy way to handle it, I have to admit.'

'So if it really comes down to a management blunder, a gross mis-estimation, why should it be us who are hauled up to pay the price?'

'The firm will have to lower costs.' John Mowbray replied cautiously.

'But that's stupid. I don't know about you, but I've never worked harder in my life than over the last three months. I've got a baby at home and a husband with no regular income. I'm hardly going to rest with my heels up. I'm beginning to get the sense that they've no idea what they're doing.'

'You can't expect Drinkwater to know how every individual has performed. We're all head office staff. At the end of the day we're not bringing in the money. That makes us overhead.'

'If that's how they view us, then why the hell did they take us on in the first place?'

'At least Drinkwater has the decency to see us all individually. It may not be as bad as you think.'

Joan Milroy had remained silent. The expression on her face was abstracted, as if her mind were very far away.

'So what have we done wrong?' Jo posed more gently after five minutes of silence.

'Wrong?' John Mowbray responded in a calm voice. 'I'm not sure we've done anything wrong.'

'Let's be honest with each other. We've all made mistakes. This situation could have been avoided, surely?'

'Avoided?'

'We're going to be here for a while. We might as well use the time to learn something from each other. Don't you think Joan?'

Joan Milroy smiled over at Jo a slow smile of disinterest.

'It's never too late to learn dear. But I don't think there's anything much I can teach you two.'

Jo carried on, ignoring her. 'Well, it seems to me the odds are two of us are going to be axed. That means one of us must somehow have played this thing right. Even if it's for posterity's sake, I'd like to know who . . .'

Step 2: Feel the five forces

The relative commercial attractiveness of any human endeavour is determined by how competitive it is. The more competitive it is the harder it will be to achieve acceptable levels of profit. A business guru called Michael Porter set out the five forces that determine the competitiveness of any market:

- What is the threat of substitution from new products?
- How high are the entry barriers to new competitors seeking to get a toehold?
- How high are the barriers for failing firms to exit gracefully without dragging everyone else down with them?
- What is the negotiating power of customers when it comes to squeezing the firm?
- What is the negotiating power of suppliers should they choose to flex their muscle?

The Five Forces model (Diagram 1) influences the way all seasoned management teams think about their competitive positioning. Like most strategic tools, it has largely remained the preserve of board level management – the generals surveying their battle lines from the ridge behind the fray.

DIAGRAM 1

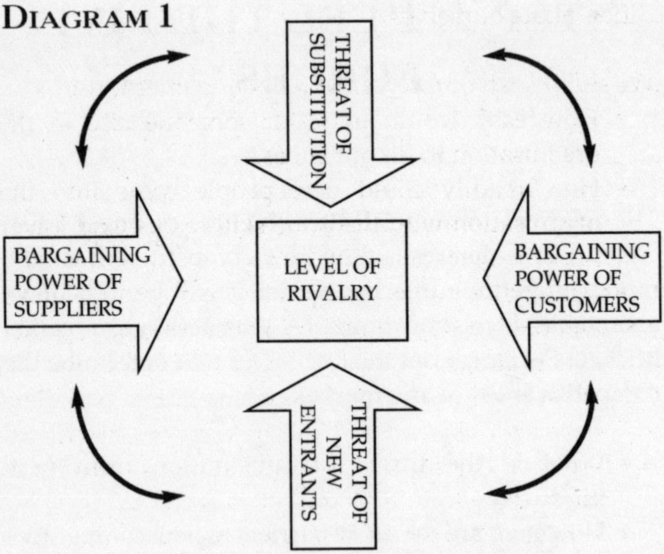

Whilst most firms ask themselves these critical questions, it is startling how rarely we ask them of ourselves. How competitive is the culture of the company where we work? What drives that competition? How should I position myself to survive and thrive?

As employees, the issue of our competitiveness is as important as it is for a firm. We compete with rivals for the respect and loyalty of our customer. We will also compete for the loyalty of our subordinates within the firm. The security of our position will depend on how easy it is for the firm to replace us, and the intensity of our rivalry with other employees will be driven in part by how established they are. How our rivals and subordinates behave will directly affect our position in the company and influence the way in which we differentiate ourselves.

We should ask ourselves the following questions:

- How easy would it be for someone else in the organisation to fill our shoes?
- How readily could new people come into the organisation with the same skills as us, and lower salary expectations?
- How good is the company at getting rid of dead wood or do we all wind up getting fired together indiscriminately?
- What level of power do our immediate superiors have over us? Can they dictate our daily activity or are they dependent on our skill and ingenuity to allow them to fulfil their own tasks?
- What level of power and influence do we have over the people who work for us? Are they loyal?

If you can be easily replaced, if there are few barriers to entry for new, cheaper recruits, if dead wood is piling up around you without your employer differentiating between you and it, and if your boss allows you no independence and your subordinates do not respect your authority, then you are highly vulnerable. If the reverse is true, then you have solid grounds on which to achieve a differentiated position within the firm.

Adopting the Five Forces view of the world of work is to accept that employment is a market-place and what matters is how efficiently we compete. It is Darwinistic.

But it is also realistic. An evaluation of your company will reveal precisely how competitive it is and what drives that competition. It may be that the chance of you ever differentiating yourself in such an environment is low, in which case you should find a more conducive setting for your talents before reality inevitably catches up with you.

Few of us bother to evaluate the competitive environment around us. We navigate through guile, intuition and luck, either good or bad. Were a business to manage itself in that fashion it would go bust within a few months. The Five Forces model is the bedrock of business strategy. It takes half an hour to master. Use it.

The takeaway

Analyse the five competitive dimensions of your workplace. If there are obvious angles of advantage (for example, you can't be readily substituted because you alone know a particular process or client), build on them. If there are areas of weakness, ask yourself how serious they are and whether the fortifications can be repaired? If they are serious you will have to compensate for them in other areas.

This methodology is your best tool for understanding the key dimensions of your competitive position. You will probably find only a tiny minority of your colleagues use it. **Feel the five forces** and stand apart from the crowd.

A TALE OF TWO DISMISSALS

There was one question Jo simply couldn't get out of her mind. Who was it that had marked her out as superfluous? Inevitably, the fact that she had gone off for three months must have had something to do with it. Somehow, despite the hard work she had invested, somewhere, somehow, a bad impression had been formed of her. She had never confronted failure in life before. It was the sheer inexplicable nature of her position that upset her most.

'He probably gets pleasure out of watching us scrap it out. It's like the Roman games. He's waiting to see who's left standing.'

'I think you're being too negative.' John Mowbray responded after a pause. 'You said yourself, a few months back everything was fine. It's not a conspiracy. It's just circumstance.'

'But you won't see top management jobs questioned. You say it's not a conspiracy, but I'll bet none of Drinkwater's cronies are being subjected to this. '

Joan Milroy smiled over at Jo. 'Did you honestly believe that there would never be competition?'

'I'm not naïve, if that's what you're implying. But you would think that once you've got a job, what matters is team work, not getting the advantage. This is not a race. We're meant to be building something together.'

'Of course, but haven't you once asked yourself who could step into your shoes?' Joan Milroy added, more insistently this time.

'I've never thought about it in that way. Why should I?'

'Ask John Mowbray. He's the one with the business degree.'

Jo turned to him and after a tense silence asked accusatorily, 'John, do you think of us as competing?'

'Not exactly.' Mowbray responded with what sounded like a derogatory laugh.

'You don't view me or anyone else as competition do you?' Jo continued more insistently.

'No, of course not.'

'And the junior people in the accounts department aren't a threat?'

'It's never crossed my mind.'

'Exactly,' Jo echoed. 'What matters in places like this is that we're all mutually supportive. Unless we worked as a team nothing would get done. That's what makes the whole thing so out of character, so bizarre.'

Joan Milroy smiled. 'You've never asked yourself if the public relations department would survive without you then?'

'Not really.' Jo replied after a pause

'Then perhaps you should have.' Joan said carefully.

'I thought you were madam morality; corporate values and all that.'

'Being ethical shouldn't be confused with not competing.'

'You've lost me Joan.'

'Part of our obligation here is to ensure we are as good as we can be, that the firm couldn't do better with someone else instead.'

'And you think you've done that?'

'I know I can't be replaced easily. No one else knows the files, or exactly how the payroll works.'

'That doesn't sound very moral Joan.'

'I do it better than anyone else. We've never missed payroll once have we? I think that makes me moral.'

'I think that makes you tragic Joan, if you really want to know. There's more to life than bloody payroll.'

Step 3: Know your value drivers

Knowing where you stand in the competitive field of your employer is not enough. Having understood the nature of competition, what matters is how and where you choose to focus your energies, and where you add value to the organisation. In the lingo of the strategists, what are your value drivers? The end goal of all firms is the creation of shareholder value. What matters is that we understand how we contribute to value creation and what therefore are our key value drivers.

'Value drivers' is probably an unfamiliar term. More conventionally you might talk about skills. The real problem with the concept of skills is that it says nothing about the impact that we have directly on the firm. We may be technically skilled but we may also deliver no value to our employer. Skills are capabilities we as individuals possess. If they don't add value to the company, they are worthless to our employer. Value drivers, by contrast, are those activities that impact on the competitiveness and profitability of the firm.

The only thing that matters to firms is how value is created. To compete effectively, you have to reframe your assessment of your own capabilities in terms of what value you bring to the firm and how you can maximise that value. The frame of reference shifts from internal to external. Instead of asking ourselves what skills we possess, we ask ourselves how we drive value. If you can do this then you are likely to be aligned with the mission of the firm which is to create shareholder value.

UNSHACKLING THE VALUE CHAINS

So this is all very interesting as a concept and all but, as one of my friends put it, where does the rubber meet the road? The starting point is to list where you believe you drive value. It may be in your ability to reduce scrap by expert tooling, it may be your ability to retain difficult customers through your sensitive negotiation style, to type at great speed whilst editing your boss's grammar, or it may be the rare quality you have of raising the morale of those around you. The initial list is likely to be long. The hard part is to cluster these attributes in a way that will guide the process of personal differentiation. To do this you need a framework: the 'Value Chain' (Diagram 2).

The Value Chain describes the areas of a firm's activity which add value to the product or service it sells. The Value Chain has come to form the basis of the way any senior executive describes the moving parts of their firm. It may be that your own contribution is isolated to one part of the value chain. But it is more probable that you have a subtle influence on a number of links in the chain, particularly if you work in a support function or as a consultant. And also the whole point of chains is that no link stands alone. Although you may toil away

DIAGRAM 2

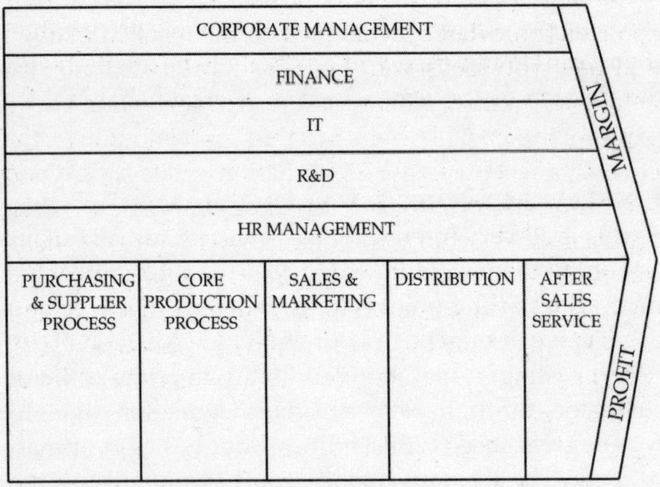

in a functional silo, the fruits of your efforts may only become apparent in other departments altogether.

It is possible you will elaborate an initial list perhaps as long as thirty value drivers, ranging from your ability to process documents accurately, to your knack of knowing how a customer is likely to react. In all probability, in no more than a couple of these are you genuinely different from your colleagues. It is here that your focus should lie. Simply by organising the thirty odd drivers into the boxes of the value chain, it is likely that they will cluster into a number of core themes. This will clearly illustrate where in the firm's underlying processes you most contribute. It is here that you are most likely to be able to differentiate yourself.

CORE COMPETENCIES

So having drilled down into the bedrock of your unique contribution, what do you do with the result? Firstly, it will help you focus your energies more tightly. It will help you hone your core value drivers, refine them, explore, and expand them. But this is not enough. At the core of any effective differentiation strategy is good communication. Whilst it is more impressive when others discover your good qualities without your help, they usually need a little reminding. Once you are clear on your value drivers, communicate them. Ensure your managers understand clearly where you add value. Speak of these competencies in terms of value drivers, of adding value. Place them firmly in the context of the firm's value chain (you will be amazed how many senior managers will have actually failed to understand the value chain of the firm at all). And also ensure that it is against these yardsticks that your performance is being evaluated.

Once learnt, the language of value drivers becomes utterly compelling. It puts everything in terms of the benefit to the firm and its customers. It isolates the critical activities of the business and makes skilled experts out of people like you and me who may previously have appeared unfocused generalists. Finding our value drivers is also finding our purpose in the life of work; something everyone from Plato on up has striven for.

The takeaway

Draw up the list of your value drivers, match them against the firm's value chain, and isolate your core competencies. (If no one has drawn up a value chain for the firm, then now is your opportunity to be the one to do so and immortalise yourself). **Know your value drivers,** for these are the hooks on which your personal strategy of differentiation will hang.

A TALE OF TWO DISMISSALS

John Mowbray had stood up and paced a couple of times round the room. Jo's comment about what an analyst actually did had clearly unnerved him. Seeing the impact was almost thrilling. She had been right to push the point, Jo reflected. What, after all, did the job of an analyst really contribute? It was an utterly nebulous title. But he clearly resented hearing it from her.

'I'm not sure I need to answer that,' he responded after a pause.

'I mean, you're the one with the big job. What is it exactly you contribute?' Jo continued.

'It's not so simple. It can't just be summarised in a sentence. It's complex. It's intellectual. We're always responding to different situations.'

'It's just I've never known what it means to be an analyst. Just one of those strange things I guess I'll never understand.' She responded half-sarcastically.

'Perhaps you find it hard to grasp because your own activities are, well, more specific.'

'You mean mundane? Beneath you?'

'You know what I mean Jo. You're the one who brought it up.'

She ignored his comment and turned to Joan Milroy who was still sitting quietly in her chair. 'Do you understand what it is he does Joan, or am I just being dense about it?'

'I've no idea. I'm a simple soul as you both know.'

'I think it's a male superiority thing. He thinks just because we can't understand it, that makes his job somehow better. I mean I understand what you do Joan and I don't think any less of you as a result.'

'Well I'm glad,' she responded ingenuously. 'I try to make it absolutely clear what I do. John Drinkwater knows precisely what I add. I make sure he knows that.'

'And that doesn't make you feel undervalued does it?' Jo added.

'Administration may not sound much to the likes of John and you. But I just want them to appreciate what I do, and not take it for granted, that's all. I know what I can add and I make sure they understand that.'

John Mowbray hesitated a moment before adding with a wry smile, 'It doesn't look like they appreciated it enough, does it?'

Step 4. Have values

'If you tell the truth, you never have to remember anything.'

In odd moments of despair it is tempting to believe that those who survive are those who will resort to any means to do so. The simplest way to make money is to rob, extort and cheat. We all hear about the fat-cats granting themselves vast stock options and pay rises whilst downsizing the companies they manage.

This cynicism tends also to affect the way we conduct our own work lives. We live in an agnostic age and the most agnostic institution of them all is the work place. Most of us are embarrassed to mention beliefs or creed. Doing so might identify us as one of the nuts, the zealots. It might also open us up to potential discrimination, to being pigeon-holed as marginal. Whilst in the personal domain we may conduct our lives along fairly well defined ethical lines, we tend to modify these in our place of work. The macho world of work calls us to do what we have to, not what we ought to do. We shed our native sense of ethics.

This is hugely ironical. Most firms are under increasing pressure to demonstrate high ethical standards. This has been driven by institutional investors who are now often required by law to demonstrate ethical investment criteria. The anti-globalisation movements, animal rights, environmental protection lobbies, might all be economically marginal but they have also brought their moral agenda to bear. Governments are being compelled to legislate ethical standards of business practice.

Few firms wish to act badly. But most firms are, however, quite unsure what being 'ethical' means. They lack the tools to make ethical judgements. Most have no ethical framework through which to filter decision making. The outcome is firms which are keen to be seen to harness ethics, but are not sure what they have to do. Therein lies a great opportunity to differentiate yourself as an employee.

WORKING FOR GOOD

In any competitive situation, she who seizes the high ground so often secures an unbeatable advantage. Ethical ground is as high as it gets. As an individual this ethical impasse at the heart of the firm presents a ripe opportunity to differentiate yourself. Exhibiting a strong sense of values is one of the surest ways to make yourself stand apart. This cannot be done cynically. If you are fundamentally unethical it will not redeem you. But provided you do have a set of values to which you subscribe – values about acceptable behaviour, about social responsibility, about accountability – then you should import them into your place of work.

If your decisions are seen to be conditioned by values, if these values are germane to the society of the firm, if they are relevant to other people employed with you, then it is unlikely you will ever be censured for using them. It is also unlikely you will ever be fired. Firing men and women of principle is something few firms dare do. People acting under a sense of principle tend to serve as magnates for others. They quickly become an unstoppable force. If they are snuffed-out they just become martyrs. That is why they are often so feared by dictators and persecutors.

What you have to do is articulate for yourself what values you hold firm to in any work-related decision. You have to make it clear that your decision making is conditioned in this way and you have to be seen to actively take an ethical stance. It does not mean being a goody-goody or sanctimonious. Nor does it mean being nice to everyone. It means conducting your work life according to clear principles which ultimately benefit the company, it's customers and fellow employees – *'I will not simply fudge this client proposal. If we can't deliver on time, it's better we confront them with it now and sort it out. I will not deceive our customers.'; 'Sure, I could pin the blame on my subordinate for the shipping error, but instead I'm going to sit down with him and work out how we can avoid it happening next time. It's my duty to do so.'*

One of the few ways any human being can achieve some degree of immortality is through becoming a beacon of values. The political, the military, the artistic, and the religious worlds have each produced such heroes, as has virtually every other vocation available to man. The one notable exception is business. When it comes to business, we can name the rich, the powerful but, with a few notable exceptions, not the good. The appeal to do what is right is an immensely powerful one. If you are clearly identified with such a decision making process you can become virtually untouchable. This does not mean continually sermonising or being a self-righteous zealot. But it does mean being identified with a moral perspective. Values in a person are as admired as they are in a firm. It is just they are like rainbows – rarely glimpsed and usually fleeting.

The takeaway

Articulate for yourself what values you believe are significant to you; whether loyalty to colleagues, making customers happy at any cost, ensuring all decisions factor in environmental issues, that weak people are treated with compassion. Then see how closely these map onto the values of the firm. If they match, then trading on the basis of these values will place you in the mainstream. If they do not, then it is likely that your own values will make you stand out. Provided these are sane, viable and commercially sound, that is no bad thing. Exercise your values visibly and vocally. Value based opinions and messages always have surprising impact and are met with tolerance rather than resistance. **Have values** and you will find you suddenly get things done and you will almost certainly be differentiated.

A TALE OF TWO DISMISSALS

To Jo it was clear that Drinkwater would be making a simple choice – between her and Joan Milroy. Either that or they would both be out together. John Mowbray had the polished veneer that marked him apart. He knew it. So did they. What was galling about the situation was that Joan Milroy was unqualified. She hadn't invested four years of her life in a college education. She was also hopelessly outdated. Whether she attended church or not Jo had no idea. But everything she did was tainted with a moral overtone. It irritated Jo intensely.

'It's my impression that you don't seem particularly resentful to be sitting here like this?' Jo had said pointedly after a long pause.

Joan Milroy shrugged. 'They wouldn't be doing this if it weren't necessary.'

'Have you thought that maybe he's messed up and he's just covering his own ass. He doesn't care what we feel. He doesn't even care what we've really contributed. We're just headcount.'

'He's a leader. All leaders must do what's right. And part of that means treating people as they deserve to be treated.'

'You're deceiving yourself if you think he cares.'

'We'll see, dear.'

'So you're willing to accept this without a fight?'

'A fight with whom? With you? With John Mowbray? As I see it, what matters is that we are given a fair hearing. And that is what he's doing as far as I can see.'

'You think this is a hearing? You can't be serious Joan.'

'Well, if it isn't, it ought to be. Everyone deserves the chance to defend their position, to argue their case.'

'That's what you'll say to him?'

'Of course. I'll make it very clear to him. I always have. We all have something to offer. Just some of us have to express it more clearly. I believe all people are essentially good, John Drinkwater included. He has to weigh the merits and contribution of each person fairly. If he doesn't then he has no right to be in charge of so many people to begin with.'

'I admire your optimism. I just don't think it applies in this case.'

'Out of this sort of mess good can come you know.'

Jo smiled. It was the sort of sanctimonious rubbish that she imagined would make a man like John Drinkwater vomit.

'What possible good are you talking about?'

'As long as he makes a fair distinction between good and bad people, then the company can move on. If he doesn't make that distinction then, as you say, it will not.'

'Good and bad. It sounds like you're expecting him to make moral judgements.'

'Jo, all judgements at heart must be moral.'

'What on earth makes someone good? Am I good? Perhaps I'm bad. I hate to say it, but it sounds hopelessly fanciful to me.'

'We all know what good people are. Drinkwater knows it too. He even gave the whole firm his list of corporate values a year ago. Remember?'

'What! That thing? You actually took it seriously? Come on Joan. Get real.'

'I took it very seriously.'

'Drinkwater probably forgot about it ten minutes after the ink was dry.'

'Then I'll remind him.'

Jo smiled.

'The fourth value was that people should be judged by their actions, not based on preference.' Joan continued.

'Joan, I don't know what to say. I think you're deluding yourself.'

'I'm going to remind him of that.'

'Rather you than me.'

Step 5: The power of being yourself

'Always remember you're unique,
just like everyone else.'

We are all ardent individualists. We are anxious to assert our idiosyncrasies at every opportunity, from our taste in wine to the cut of our clothes. If you look at the people seated around you on the train to work, none of them appear remotely the same. They have different hair cuts, glasses, their own mannerisms. Even their mobile phones have different tones. We all need to express our opinions as individuals and broadcast what makes us different. It is the power of this instinct that has undermined even the most brutal modern attempts to quash it.

The Stone Age firm

Yet, standing starkly against this current of self-expression is the firm. The overwhelming pressure in the work place is towards conformity. The primary impulse of management is towards standardisation. We have all probably experienced it, from the questions asked at our job interview, to the methods the firm uses to assess our performance.

The management of individuals at work is much like the challenge faced by marketeers. Mass marketing, which assumes homogenous customer needs, is far easier to administer. But the future is one-to-one marketing. Of course, one-to-one marketing is frankly a pain in the ass. It is the same with talented employees. The hardest part of management is dealing with individual egos. Like customers, we all have to be treated uniquely if we are to be developed and retained. However, most firms do not even make the attempt.

Most firms adopt a low cost strategy to human resource management. They limit spend on training to an average of one per cent of revenue. The HR department is usually something of a stagnant backwater. Opinions are not sought, evaluation systems are rigid. The only firms that are the exception to the rule, and consistently adopt a differentiated approach to developing their people, are those firms whose assets ride the elevator out of the building every evening – the professional service firms such as McKinsey or Goldman Sachs. But the professional service community only serves as home to a small minority of the total labour market. That leaves the ninety per cent of the rest of us.

MAKING A STAND

The fact that management science is premised on the mass marshalling of human capital does not mean that it would be a wise personal strategy to go along with it. Keep your strategic goal constantly in your mind – to obtain the holy grail of personal differentiation. Complying unthinkingly with dominant management processes is to pursue a low cost strategy.

The decision to run against the grain and assert your individuality is not an easy one. Low cost appears low risk. But surrender is also a recipe for personal vulnerability. As soon as you can no longer be distinguished from your co-workers then you are a cost not an asset.

So how can you remain yourself and defend or even enhance your position against a tide of conformity? The over-riding management impetus of any firm is towards uniformity. Yet, all firms have an equally strong thirst for individuals who can inspire, who can spark the machine into action. Individuals tend to get valued for what they personally bring to the party, not for their willingness to accede to a process.

Individualism is needed throughout any organisation. It need not imply loss of control by the management team. It can simply mean someone offering a compelling, inspiring point of view, a locus of energy for others to emulate. This, for lack of a better term, could be called 'thought leadership'.

TOWARDS THOUGHT LEADERSHIP

If individuality is a key component of differentiation, the question is how to make it productive rather than disruptive. What guises should it take, what colours should it show? Do flares help? What about writing with the left hand or using a quill pen in meetings? How about a pince-nez? This is all fashion. It has its role but it is not what really differentiates us. The currency of modern commerce is ideas and innovation – doing something in a way no one has done before and perhaps with altogether new results. If other people adopt those ideas, you become a thought leader.

If there is one thing that the majority of firms lust after like nothing else, it is innovation. It is like five-year-olds and McDonalds – all whiney and pleading. The reason is simple and entirely rational. Firms have to differentiate themselves and to differentiate they have to innovate. Innovation does not simply mean inventing a new product or service. The bulk of innovation occurs in the way products and services are created. Productivity improvements are the engine of economic growth.

A decade ago the average large firm could probably rest on its laurels if it produced one significant innovation every three to five years. This sort of pace would now be perceived as positively indolent. Unless a firm can innovate significantly every two years and continually produce incremental innovation in the meantime, it will quickly fall out of favour with investors. The conveyor belt is speeding up.

This of course poses a serious challenge for most firms. Where do they get the continual flow of ideas? What is the source of inspiration? The traditional answer has been the research and development department. Because R&D people were not typically mainstream, they were locked away from the main flows of the firm lest they infect it with their mad-hatterliness. The result was often ideas that could not practically be implemented by the firm, and a sluggish, backed-up pipeline of innovation.

The only answer, like most answers, lies within. When exposed to a problem, most of us come up with ideas. We all, if unfettered, have our own opinions. That's what makes us unique. The problem is that, having placed a premium on conformity, firms have ensured that most employees are not capable of standing outside the flow sufficiently to see beyond it. We are not only incapable of seeing the wood for the trees, we are the trees. We are all stuck in someone else's model.

THINKING DIFFERENT

There is a useful tool to get us out of this blind alley, and to help us put our individuality to good use – 'triangulation'. When looking at a problem, triangulation requires the formation of three mental points. At one point stands the process or system as it currently operates. At another stands the you as part of that process, the docile employee towing the company line. At the third point stands your true identity, assessing the problem at hand. This third perspective is one where all your spirit of individuality is let out. Your creative juices are free to flow. Your instincts are given full reign. You are at home, feet up on the kitchen table, holding forth (Diagram 3).

How does the real you see things differently? How can you criticise your false, company self? Drawing on all the resources of your individuality, how can you reinvent beyond the company mantra? Triangulation produces a new solution to every problem, quite distinct from the answer you might customarily propose. The solution may not be correct but it will act as a reality check on received wisdom. Just be yourself and apply your individuality to the situation where otherwise you would simply mimic the company orthodoxy. That will make you a thought leader. Triangulate. Constructive individualists rarely get fired.

DIAGRAM 3

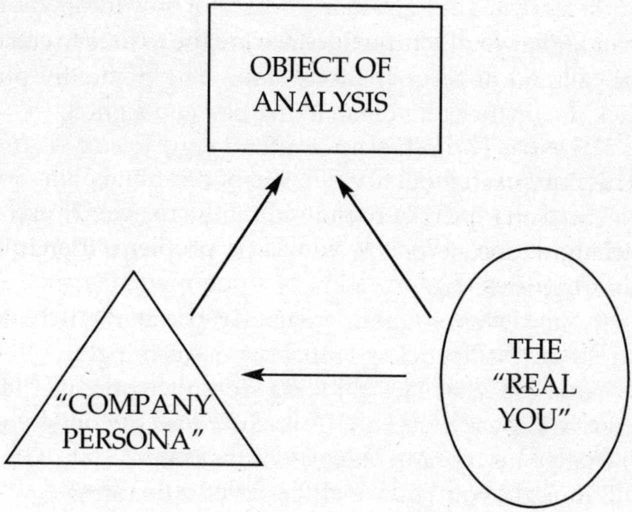

The takeaway

You have a unique perspective to offer your employer, but every survival instinct will be telling you that you must conform. So how do you escape the straightjacket without being branded a rebel? Triangulate. Experiment with a personalised, alternative viewpoint that reflects your own character more than any company orthodoxy. See if this process generates constructive ideas. If it does, then you will be a thought leader. **The power of being yourself** will be unleashed.

A TALE OF TWO DISMISSALS

Joan Milroy finally turned to face Jo, just in time to catch the tail-end of a supercilious smile. She pointedly put back the lipstick and blush in her bag and sighed.

'I'm sorry. I didn't mean to offend you,' Jo added after an awkward silence.

'You don't have to apologise. I know people find me somehow amusing. I'm not sure why really, but it doesn't bother me.'

'It's just I was wondering what Drinkwater will think. Bright purple lipstick is probably not his thing.'

'You see, what he's thinking doesn't worry me. He already knows what I am. A few minutes are not going to change his opinion one way or the other.'

'I thought you said we all deserved a hearing?'

'That's right. But I have no interest in defending myself. What have I done that needs defending?'

'So there'll just be silence?'

'No. I'm more interested in him than me. Think how he must be viewing the situation. He built the firm up over twenty years from scratch. I saw him do it and it wasn't easy. Every time he sees the people working here he must feel a pang of pride. And now he has to cut a piece out of his baby. It must hurt.'

'Don't tell me you're going to try and counsel him?'

'No. Just sympathise.'

'I think you're misreading the man, the situation. He will think you're acting bizarrely.'

'I'll be myself. I always am.'

Jo smiled. 'I don't understand you Joan, I'm sorry.'

'In this sort of situation it's too easy to only think of

yourself. But we're expecting John Drinkwater to think about us. It seems to me that he's probably feeling as bad as we are or perhaps even worse. It can't be easy. If there's one way for good to come of this, it's for him to know he's not alone. None of us are alone. I've been here from the beginning. The saddest day would be to see it all end. I want him to know that.'

'I still don't understand you Joan. I shouldn't have even raised it I guess. My fault.'

Step 6. Know your own worth

Worth is founded on perception and reinforced by social stereotype. Why do we value diamonds so highly when their only practical application is drill-heads? Why has man always killed for gold when it is probably one of the few substances on earth that is utterly useless?

Worth is a transactional concept. It exists as a function of the tradability of one object for another, useless or otherwise. We determine the relative worth of two objects through experimental exchange. When enough people think something similar about the value of an object then a stable market is established.

All markets become stable when demand and supply are in some sort of equilibrium. A stable market usually presupposes that there are a number of suppliers and a number of buyers. The existence of a single buyer, or alternatively a single supplier, usually leads to market distortion, to unpredictable pricing. Either side can manipulate the value as they wish.

The value attached to time and energy follows the same laws as those that apply to gold and diamonds. All are valued because there is a market for them. We trade our time and energy for cash, a pension and other psychological benefits. But, unlike the market for diamonds, in a stable employment situation, there is only one bidder for your time and energy – your employer. Their single-minded aim is to avoid bidding against themselves. The larger market exists beyond the firm and occasionally, as an employee threatens to leave, the two markets interact. But forcing them to interact is never a comfortable thing to bring about and often only occurs when you have one foot already out of the door. The challenge for us as employees is to impose a reality check but without having to go to the wire by threatening to leave.

The best way to check your own worth, without ultimatums, is to use a headhunter. Firms use headhunters to poach good people, but in so doing perpetuate a cycle whereby their employees are in turn poached. Employees, like their employers, have an ambivalent relationship with headhunters. Some industries accept them as a norm, such as advertising, investment banking and IT. Such industries are characterised by high levels of employee churn. But for most sectors the only heads that get hunted are those of directors. Assuming you are not a director, this can pose problems when you want to put your finger on the pulse of the market. Nevertheless some sort of check should be possible.

An understanding of your market value is invaluable when negotiating a firm position with your employer that is mutually rewarding. If you do not know your own worth, then it is impossible to judge whether others are doing so correctly or how you should influence their opinions. Firms competing for customers do it all the time. It is called benchmarking. Benchmarking is one of the underpinnings of modern strategy and it should also be a foundation stone of your personal strategy.

THINK VALUE PRICING

Most firms encourage employees to measure their rewards and performance against an internal rather than an external standard. The reason is obvious. If employees turn their eyes outward, the firm simply winds up having to compete with the market for resources it believes it already controls.

Often a firm will genuinely be unaware of your market worth. If you know what this should be and communicate it effectively, it is likely you will be able to prompt a correction. Of course, it is best to start the other way round – set a price and leave it up to the firm to find a way to justify this to itself. This is called 'value pricing'. This is the staple mechanic of branding. Set the figure at what you believe is fair and right and you will have created an expectation in the mind of your employer that you are worth it. Price can send the clearest possible signal about value. That is why it is called value pricing.

If this all seems too pushy, reflect on this. How can you seriously expect others to value you if you do not know your own worth? A sense of value leads to a whole set of subtle communications that tend to reinforce your position. In essence, using a headhunter or researching what competitors pay is like doing personal market research, and will strengthen your position enormously. Know your value and act on this knowledge.

The takeaway

As with all markets, things move quickly in the employment market. On at least an annual basis you should understand where you stand in terms of value and marketability. If the market tells you you are in decline, then it is time to act before someone else reads the tea leaves. If you are over compensated, then you had better build your brand fast to justify your cost – **know your own worth** or you will get in trouble.

A TALE OF TWO DISMISSALS

'So you're saying you could get more elsewhere? Then why on earth have you stuck around?' Jo responded incredulously. She couldn't believe John Mowbray was serious. 'You're honestly saying you'd do the job even if they cut your salary?' she continued in a sceptical tone.

'I didn't join for the money. Communicopia's probably one of the best places to get experience in this industry. Drinkwater's a god. I don't have a family yet, so it's a trade-off I could afford to make. That's all I'm saying.'

'Are you going to tell him that?' Jo continued.

'Well, I suppose I might as well, if it comes to it. I think it'll make my commitment pretty clear at least.'

Joan Milroy smiled at Jo. 'You look worried.'

'Well, I guess its true. I am.'

'You think you're overpaid then?'

'Well, not exactly. Just before I came back from maternity leave I looked around. I wanted to see what other people were paying.'

'And you negotiated a raise.'

'Well, yes. It seemed the right thing to do. Until now of course.'

Joan Milroy didn't respond. John Mowbray was staring at Jo intently. 'How much are we talking? Twenty per cent?' Then, after a pause, 'Thirty?'.

Jo still didn't respond.

'Forty per cent?' he continued.

Jo involuntarily smiled. She couldn't help it.

'I don't believe it.' Mowbray suddenly snapped. 'Jesus, I've been here for two years and I haven't had a single raise. I could double my salary in the City.'

'Then why didn't you?' Joan Milroy interceded in an abstracted tone.

'Well, now I guess I'm glad I didn't push. At least I'm not an overhead like some people I could name.'

Jo turned away to hide the deep blush that had spread up her neck and into her cheeks.

STEP 7. DON'T BE AFRAID TO BE HIGH COST

So, we are agreed: there is no absolute value. Value is created by the existence of a market, and all markets are driven by mutual perception. Because we perceive something to be of value, we value it. Value creates value.

We return once more to our initial choice of personal strategies – whether to be low cost or to seek to differentiate ourselves. When it comes to salary negotiation it is easy to assume that the low cost route is the safe route. Keep your head below the parapet and it won't get shot off. If your cost doesn't even make it onto the corporate radar screen, you are unlikely to be in the spotlight. But of course, the price you demand and command sends important signals about your value. A whole set of perceptions are set in motion. And your intuitive assumptions about how these perceptions work may not be correct.

It is a peculiar quirk of pricing strategy that cheap products tend also to command low customer loyalty. In other words, there is little emotion involved in dumping one for another. Low value breeds low loyalty. If you buy something based on cost, you will switch for the same reason.

This fact produces some counter-intuitive logic. In a downturn, when costs have to be cut, logic would suggest that those on big salaries would be the first to go. Big salaries should mean obvious fat to cut.

Unfortunately things do not work that way. Obvious corporate fat is indeed an easy cut. But it is usually lower- and mid-salaried employees that bear the brunt of most downsizing. The reason for the paradox is that salary is a prime indicator of worth. If you get paid more you are construed to be worth more. The more you are perceived to be worth the more reluctant a firm will be to remove you, even if your actual value added is not the greatest. People on big pay cheques are assumed to be mission critical. Those on low salaries, the logic goes, can be easily substituted.

As an employee, being in this low cost position is a very vulnerable one. You need to send a strong signal about your value by being paid appropriately. In a downturn it is the differentiated crew who stay in the boat. A proportion of the rest drown without trace or ceremony, just like the second class passengers on the Titanic.

AWAY WITH FALSE MODESTIES

Most of us are intensely bashful about seeking pay rises or renegotiating contracts. We typically wait to receive them. And if we feel under-rewarded we usually try to move jobs rather than manage the uncomfortable process of confrontation. However, negotiating constructively during the good times about salary is a vital plank to building perceptions of your worth. It is not something to be bashful about. Whether the rise is a big one or small is not the point. What matters is the signal any increment sends. You should always be aiming to achieve a raise above the company average each year and prepare evidence showing why you are worth it. If you succeed, you will be deemed to have added value.

The takeaway

View salary as a competitive tool, and one that is key to the process of differentiation. Ensure you always nudge at least marginally ahead of your peer group; prepare a careful analysis of your value drivers as justification. Sell yourself as hard to the firm as the firm sells itself to its customers. **Don't be afraid to be high cost.** At the end of the day you are a product. The question is, how good is your brand? That's where we go next.

A TALE OF TWO DISMISSALS

'Don't tell me you've done the same thing Joan?'

'What do you mean John?'

'Screwed the company for every penny you could get out of it.'

'As I said before, I know what I'm worth. I may not have studied economics but I know what inflation means. It is only right they should raise my salary each year.'

'Each year Joan? You're saying you've got an annual payrise. No one gets that.'

'Well I do.'

'You and Jo between you. God knows how many people in the company have been playing the same game. I had no idea this sort of thing was going on.'

'John, I have a feeling we're the exception, not the rule.' Joan responded curtly. 'Perhaps I should never have mentioned it.'

'I'm not so sure. I'm beginning to understand why the company's in trouble. I wonder if Drinkwater realises what's been happening.'

'You're going to raise it with him?'

'Maybe.'

'I think you're making a mistake. It will just sound like sour grapes.'

'Perhaps. We'll see won't we.'

Step 8: Think brand equity

At some point in its evolution, any product, service or firm that is seeking to differentiate itself will need to develop a brand. A brand is that bundle of intangible qualities that add up to the worth of something and validates our perception. We are all experts at identifying, evaluating and making use of brands. As consumers we are all brand literate in a way that no previous generation could ever have dreamt of being. Yet despite this expertise, we pay remarkably little attention to honing our own brand.

Like it or not, we all have a personal brand. Part of it we inherit from our place of birth and the values of our parents, whether we be Essex man or East Coast WASP. But mostly our brand is conditioned by how we choose to lead our lives and interact with other people. An important element of our worth is wrapped up with our brand. It may sound appallingly superficial, but peoples' brands are the primary indicators we all use to make judgements about others. *'Dick's the intellectual type, smart but impractical. Samantha's the smiley sort, no substance or sincerity.'*

A fundamental part of our brand is how 'with it', how 'hip', or conscious of trends we appear. This does not simply relate to the cut of one's shirt or skirt, but it is bound up with persona, presence, values and judgement. Above all, it relates to how in tune we are with our market. Again, we have to think of ourselves as a company. A firm whose brand is perceived to be out of touch, passé, tarnished, will quickly fade from favour.

Being able to adapt to culture as it evolves around us is important. The phrase that usefully encapsulates this state of sensitivity is 'early adopter' – someone who is open-minded and curious about new products and services, and easily adapts to buying and using them. Becoming an early adopter is a strategy, not simply a skill. It requires being sensitised to major trends, working out their relevance to you, and what you do, and adapting yourself to take advantage of them. In the context of work, it means bringing-in new ideas in a way that will get a constructive response, whether it be the repositioning of an existing product or the creation of an entirely new one.

Once you focus on early adoption of external trends, this is likely to highlight the relative inertia of your employer. Most firms are lamentably slow to assimilate changes of fashion in the larger world around them. There is an ingrained conservativeness to any institution built on a fabric of internal customs and rules. So much of the average firm's energy is inward facing and the larger the firm becomes the more that dynamic holds true. Although many of the individuals involved may be fully aware of changes in the larger world, collectively groups of people are slow to react. Management so often calls out for change but the world around them is in reality changing far faster than they realise. Customers are often ahead of producers.

GET WITH IT . . .

Unusually, this puts you, the individual, at a potential advantage over your employer. The strategy of early adoption has served innovative firms well. The same strategy works equally well for the individual. If you can assimilate trends faster than the firm and communicate them effectively in a way that promotes change, you will very clearly stand out from the crowd.

Becoming identified as an early adopter is not as hard as it sounds. In all aspects of your life outside work you have exposure to social change. Your children will often pick-up on them first in the playground – from mobile phones, to shifts in favoured colours, to evolving views towards sex. Kids drove the explosion in text messaging and they also inspired the renaissance of backpacks. They are often the first assimilators of new phrases and modes of expression. As spotty teenagers, they are the main consumers of cultural fashions. It should not after all be that surprising. Kids see the world through new, unjaundiced eyes. All innovation needs a new lens.

Also never overestimate the simple, very human processes by which firms keep in touch with their markets. Firms can appear to be impregnable monoliths driven by scientific principles. In reality, like all societies, they turn to early adopters to get their bearings about where the world will turn next. Ideas come from small, improbable sources; snippets of conversation, a sample left on a marketing director's desk. Many management teams make the arrogant assumption that the firm generates ideas and then passes these on to consumers. That is not usually how it works. Firms do not have ideas. People have ideas. And they usually get those ideas from observing normal life. This is how most great consumer inventions come into being, from Post It notes to roller-blades. Once you are perceived as an early adopter, you will have strengthened your brand immeasurably.

The takeaway

Make it a matter of discipline to observe new trends outside your work life and categorise them. Every month or two, reshuffle what you have observed and see if any could have a bearing on the firm's products or processes. If you make this a key part of what you do, you will become an inadvertent leader of change and recognised as making a unique contribution. **Think brand equity**.

A TALE OF TWO DISMISSALS

John Mowbray was looking increasingly irritated and anxious. For the past fifteen minutes Joan Milroy had been punching the miniaturised keypad of her mobile phone, and every few seconds the silence was punctuated by a sharp bleep. Eventually, Mowbray got to his feet and began to pace up and down the long room, his heels clicking on the wooden surface.

'It's one thing I've never understood,' he said acerbically. 'How people can use mobiles in public places oblivious of everyone around them. They do it all the time on my train to Waterloo. It drives me nuts.'

Joan Milroy didn't respond but continued pressing the buttons intently.

'I hope it's something important. Strange time to be playing with your phone don't you think?' he continued.

'It's my grandson. I don't know whether or not you consider that important. We text message each other once a day.'

'Your grandson?' John Mowbray stared at her with bemusement.

'You don't have to look at me like I'm a dinosaur. Yes, I have a grandson. He's only six but he gets it better than me.'

'I'm not sure this is the place.'

'Of course it is. This is a communications company isn't it? That's what I'm doing – communicating.'

'I think that's a somewhat fanciful connection to make.'

'Not at all. Text messaging is a serious marketing tool

you know. Oliver's only six but he's shown me how to do it.'

'Perhaps you should get Drinkwater to answer him next time.'

'I doubt he knows how. I'd have to teach him.'

'And no doubt you will, if he gives you half a chance.'

'You're right. Perhaps I should,' she answered after pondering the idea. 'I'm sure it's one of the real problems around here. We're too obsessed with counting the beans and not enough with creating ideas. That's what John Drinkwater always said this business is about. Ideas. I'm beginning to think my grandson has more ideas than all of us put together.'

Step 9. Cultivate a Personal Myth

Myth is central to our sense of worth. Myth feeds aspiration and desire. It is the pursuit of myth that drives our inventive instincts. It is also what draws us so irresistibly to historical figures, half lost in the mists of memory, from Billy the Kid to Joan of Arc.

Myth is also the underpinning of branding. At the core of every great brand is a myth. Brands act through aspiration – the impression of value that comes from an idea with which we long to identify. That is why De Beers ads always slinkily allude to James Bond-like seductions. It is why SUVs with their call to the wild, rugged man in all Americans, have shifted more volume than any other automobile in history. Malboro Man is the cowboy hero stalking through every male psyche.

When it comes to corporate branding, firms are often quite skilled exploiters of myth. Typically, the myth is based on a founding father, a human spirit of gutsy inventiveness that set the firm on its track. Virgin Group has Branson's discovery of Tubular Bells from a phone booth in North London. Hewlett Packard has the image of its eponymous founders tinkering away at a primitive computer in their suburban garage. Autonomy Corporation was allegedly brought to life amid the cigar smoke of an Oxford pub. All such stories contribute to the myth, to the corporate brand, and many of us are drawn towards them as a result, both as employees, customers and investors.

But, although we respond so readily to it, we are far slower to cultivate the power of myth for our own benefit. Myth does not come to people easily. This has been compounded by the fact that most people are intensely uncomfortable about standing out from the crowd. It is a fundamental aspect of human psychology that we favour close identification with groups. Being exposed as different has its risks.

Personal myth is therefore usually the preserve of CEOs and founding chairmen. The heads of companies are typically voracious users of the media. Every opportunity is seized upon. Many businesses are founded on the cult of the personal myth, from Ferragamo to Jack Welch's GE. The individual and the business become indivisible. As investors or employees we look to idols, the same as we do on the screen.

TELLING TALES

But there is no monopoly on myth. The archetypal myth is afterall that of the ordinary man made good. To differentiate yourself successfully you have to cultivate personal equity (Step 8). One element of personal equity is myth. What is there about you which makes you unusual, that shows your qualities to which other employees can aspire? How can you make yourself memorable against the clutter of fellow workers, each with better pressed suits and whiter smiles? What is there from your past that marks you out? A fortunate escape, some heroic deed, a formative event? We are all storytellers at heart. You should not be afraid to develop good stories about yourself.

In work life, people quickly get categorised. This usually happens on the basis of one or two snippets of information. It is a terrible way of pigeon-holing people, but we are all guilty of it. In the fleeting encounters of contemporary life we only have time to look for small signals. It is because of this that myth and story telling can play such a decisive role in personal branding. If you have a story that reflects your myth that is how you will be understood and pigeon-holed. So make sure it's a good one, because once established it's pretty much impossible to reverse.

The takeaway

You know what your value drivers are. You've decided how you want to be branded. Think of a story from your past that embodies those qualities. Repeat it a few times and you will give rise to your own myth. *'Jane is the woman who climbs mountains in her spare time. You can be sure she will tackle this client with the same grit it took to conquer the foothills of Nepal.'* We all remember stories and myth. **Cultivate a personal myth**.

A TALE OF TWO DISMISSALS

Jo was standing with her hands pressed against the cold glass of the window. A barge was slowly fighting its way against the current towards Lambeth Bridge. For a moment she imagined herself standing on it, the wind sharp against her face, the sense of an unknown world opening up ahead of her. For a brief instant she wondered what it would be like to let herself fall. Then she pulled herself back. Joan Milroy had carefully laid a hand on her arm.

'I know what you're feeling.' Joan said gently.

Jo turned and smiled at her. 'I'm sorry for being so aggressive. It's just not easy is it? This I mean.'

'Things really aren't as bad as you may think.'

'You're right. I know. Actually, I was just thinking how irrelevant it all is.'

'What do you mean?'

'How, five minutes after I've left the building, no one will remember who I was, what I did. I will have left no mark, just a few memos still circulating round the intranet. I don't know why I care about this place at all, whether I stay or go.'

'You're being too negative. You're too hard on yourself.'

'You think so?'

'Of course. You've made your mark on the firm. Didn't you know?'

Jo looked at her blankly.

'You're the only woman who's come back three months after having a child. None of the other women in the place can understand how you did it.'

Jo shrugged.

'You shouldn't underestimate the impression your commitment has made. Everyone knows the story.'

'I hadn't even thought about it that way.'

'If I were you, I wouldn't either,' John Mowbray chimed in.

'Why John?' Joan Milroy replied sharply. 'Does the idea of being outshone by a woman really scare you that much?'

Mowbray didn't respond. On reflection he decided it was not worth the effort. He was just glad Drinkwater would probably say it for him.

Step 10. It's called marketing . . .

In an age of brands, as much value is created through communication as it is through manufacture or service. That is why we reach for Evian and not tap water. We are all experts at interpreting brand communications. We are so honed through years of exposure that decoding brand messages is a skill that has become instinctive. We each take in an average of a month of branded messages a year. That's almost as much time as we spend eating.

Communication lies at the heart of all brands. This makes it all the more bizarre that when it comes to our personal brand, most of us don't take communication that seriously. Like breathing, it is something we all take so for granted that we don't reflect on how central it is to our competitive position.

By contrast, the average firm is intensely focused on managing communications. Most firms commit on average seven per cent of their revenues to the effort of communicating their brands (compared to the one per cent devoted to developing human resources!). The marketing director controls perhaps the largest single budget item in the firm, and it is customer facing strategy that dictates the corporate agenda of most companies. The four P's of product, price, position and promotion ring out their evangelical chant like a corporate heartbeat. All the famous firms you could care to mention have grown so through effective marketing. It is hard to accuse most firms of not taking marketing seriously.

Conversely, most of us employees are guilty of complacency. Few of us view communication as something we have to manage actively. We rarely have a strategy for what we want to communicate, to whom, when and how. Communication is just one of those things that happens, like the twang of harp strings when you turn on your computer. Working life is not a marketing event.

The weakness of introversion in a consumer society is that the market can all too easily move past you as you navel gaze and leave you spinning redundantly in its wake. Failing to be marketing oriented as an employee is dangerous. You don't last.

VIVA VOCE . . .

As with all business processes, there is a well-established and simple methodology to marketing:

1. **Who**: you have to understand your target audience and tailor your message accordingly
2. **What**: you have to understand how this audience is likely to interpret your message and how best you can communicate it to achieve acceptance
3. **How**: you craft the message to suit your media and await the perfect time to broadcast it

This all requires some forethought. It is called a marketing plan. All companies have them, and virtually none of us employees do. It's a simple logic to adopt when communicating your value drivers or any other benefit you bring to an organisation.

Marketing is the most basic act of self creation. Without a voice, you are nothing. By communicating, you exist as an entity for the company. The more you communicate, and the more consistently you do so, the more likely it is your message will get through. The Vermeers and Keats' of this world, made famous by their fleeting epiphanies, are few and far between. Unless you market yourself actively and voluminously you will be a statistic in the mass of the cost-based corporate body.

The takeaway

The elements of your personal marketing plan are quite simple when seen in relation to your work on your value drivers. The core qualities to communicate are derived from your value drivers. You have to ask yourself: who is your communications best targeted at, what is the best method of communication, how often should you hit them and how do you intend to measure the results? This calls for a plan. Get planning. **It's called marketing** . . .

A TALE OF TWO DISMISSALS

'I'm just amazed it doesn't embarrass you, that's all,' John Mowbray smiled.

'Really? I don't find it embarrassing. It's just part of me. We've been married for almost thirty years now. Neither of us could have imagined then something like that would happen to us. But he got cancer, and we had to cope. I want people to know that caring for people matters to me. It's what I am. I care for people here too.'

'But it's like you want everyone to know about it – the photo on your desk, the continued references. I saw you even wrote an article about it on the company website. 'Caring for people', or something like that.'

'That's what I'm about John – caring for people. It's what I enjoy. And I think it makes a firm like Communicopia a better place.'

'But dragging your personal life into work . . .' John Mowbray continued.

They sat in silence for a moment before Joan turned to John Mowbray; 'What I find strange, John, is that I know nothing about you. If someone asked me "what does John Mowbray stand for?" I couldn't tell them. I don't even know if you have a fiancée, if you're a chess master or a plane spotter. I think that's more odd John, than people knowing you've got a sick husband. When no one knows what or who you are. When you don't seem to care about anything in particular.'

'We're here to work Joan, not to make people happy. That's what men like Drinkwater value. He wants results. I get results.'

'What results John? This? A company in trouble?'

'No one cares about your compassion Joan. I hate to sound cruel, but you shouldn't kid yourself.'

'I never kid myself. You're kidding yourself if you think what you are doesn't matter. It does.'

'What can I say Joan . . .'

Step 11. Speak the Lingo

None of us fare well in an environment where we do not speak the language. We order tea instead of coffee, ask for a donkey instead of butter (*burro* means butter in Italian, but in a Spanish bar you would be redirected to the local donkey stables!). Language defines the community we belong to more emphatically than anything else, even colour. All areas of human endeavour have their language. Flautists and composers speak in quavers, physicists converse in quantum mechanics, hunters in braces and kills, sailors in yardarms and fathoms. The same is true of firms.

What is the common language of companies? English you might naturally assume? Not so. The only universal language of firms is numbers. The language of numbers is far more pervasive than any national language. Its roots are in a lexicon called 'generally accepted accounting practice' or GAAP and, although this varies marginally by country, its fundamental grammar is pretty much universal.

The language of accounting is the seminal germ of all corporate language. But, from it has evolved a linguistic form which is contemporary, popular and more practical. This is the language of finance. It is probably not a language you are familiar with. Few employees of firms speak the language of finance. It is an elitist language, the preserve of senior management and the beneficiaries of MBA courses.

This same pattern of linguistic exclusivity has repeated itself in most societies, through from ancient Babylonia to modern day Québec. The top dogs speak one language, the workers another. It is one of the most fundamental tokens of social hierarchy. As with any sort of illiteracy, financial illiteracy is a fundamental obstacle to progression and security.

Most importantly, the language of finance is a universal one. This makes it incredibly powerful, particularly in the context of increasingly globalised firms. By contrast the language used by us employees in firms tends to be localised and situational. The language we speak is analogous to the old provincial dialects. This means us local folk are often marginalised from participation in company-wide language and the wider business community. We are prevented from taking part in the debates that matter. We sound parochial and ill-informed. As a result, we all too readily slide into the realm of the low cost mentality. That is not a comfortable place to be.

THE LANGUAGE GULF

Like strategy, the key financial indices of any business are usually known by remarkably few people. As an employee you are likely to have some inkling of how the overall business is actually doing. You will have a sense, an intuition, but typically little more, and your observations may not hold true across the entire firm. It is an issue to which firms are often extraordinarily insensitive.

This results, not surprisingly, in a fundamental tension. On the one hand management will be trying to make the firm respond based on data they are scrutinising daily. On the other, the people who can make things happen typically do not have the information they need to guide their actions. It is this impasse that brings most change programmes to a grinding halt.

NO NUMBER IS BORING . . .

Numbers are boring and unpleasant, at least that's the misperception. The language of finance can infact be interesting and uncomplicated. It certainly does not require a PhD. The financial numbers that matter with any business are infact incredibly simple. After all, they have to be simple enough for a finance director to explain to a board of non-executive directors most of whom have no detailed understanding of the business.

If everything else is stripped away, there are only three financial measures which really matter:

1. Share price, or value per share, is a simple measure. Often people refer to the market capitalisation of a firm rather than its share price. This is simply the number of shares in existence, multiplied by the share price. It is a measure of a firm's overall value.
2. Earnings-per-share of the firm or its EPS. This is the after-tax earnings of the firm divided by the number of shares in existence. It is a measure of

how much profit goes to each shareholder.

3. The price earnings multiple or PE. This is the market capitalisation or value of the firm divided by its after-tax earnings. It measures how the markets regard the firm based on its earnings performance and its prospective growth. The faster a firm's earnings are growing the higher its PE will be.

Armed with market cap, EPS and the PE, you have all the basic equipment you need to understand how the firm is performing from a financial standpoint. It really is that simple – teach yourself finance in ten seconds (Diagram 4).

DIAGRAM 4

Share Price × Shares in Issue = **Market Capitalisation**

Market Capitalisation ÷ Earnings = **PE**

Earnings ÷ Shares in Issue = **EPS**

The takeaway

The language of finance is likely to be the easiest language you've ever learnt. Put aside the teenage nightmares of classroom French or German exams. This language is simple and infinitely more powerful. It has three core phrases; market cap, EPS and PE. Any on-line service will quote the three metrics for any quoted stock. Read them, follow them, familiarise yourself with them. In all interactions with the management of your firm demonstrate clear understanding of how the actions of your department influence these outcomes. **Speak the lingo** of finance and you will discover a new range of people will be prepared to listen to what you are saying – people who matter.

A TALE OF TWO DISMISSALS

'I wonder what's going through Drinkwater's head right now,' Jo asked rhetorically after a long pause in the conversation. 'He's probably preoccupied whether he'll get down to his villa in France before the winter; whether he'll get that last sail in down at Cowes. The sort of stuff that we couldn't even dream of worrying about. The last thing on his mind is probably us.'

'You read the papers, don't you?' John Mowbray asked pointedly after she had stopped.

'I'm in PR. Of course I read the papers. I probably read more papers in a day than you guys in finance read in a year.'

'Then, you'll know the answer to your own question.'

'What do you mean?'

'Turn to the back page of the *Financial Times*.'

Jo looked back at him with a blank, suspicious look.

'That's probably the only thing he's focused on this morning.' John Mowbray continued.

'What do you mean, John? You're talking gobble-degook.'

'It lists all the PE's.'

'The what?' Jo snapped back irritably. She couldn't stand John Mowbray's condescending tone.

'The price earnings ratio. Communicopia is down at twelve. The sector average is sixteen.'

'That's bad I suppose.'

'Very bad.'

'Maybe so, but I'd still bet Drinkwater's thinking about his villa in Provence. Not everyone thinks like you John.'

Step 12. Think, live, breathe share price

'The quickest way to double your money is to fold it in half and put it back in your pocket'

Make no mistake about it, the only reason the modern firm is in business is to enrich shareholders. This means maximising the share price and the market capitalisation of the company. The share price is driven by the growth in earnings-per-share of the company. The faster the earnings-per-share are growing, the greater the valuation attached to the company. The valuation of the company is, as we know, measured in terms of the market multiple (otherwise known as its 'rating'). This is the market capitalisation divided by its after-tax earnings, (or its share price divided by its earnings-per-share). This is the basis on which firms are compared. The faster the growth rate the firm can achieve, the greater the multiple it will attract. This is why shareholders focus so devotedly on growth in earnings above all else.

The increase in shareholder power has been one of the major causes of the explosion of management fads, from downsizing, to rightsizing, to core competencies. The need to satisfy shareholder hunger for regular earnings growth inevitably prompts a continual flow of management initiatives to increase profitability. A thousand paradigms have been born, each with a life span of nine months. No wonder work can at times feel like trench warfare.

CROSSING THE SHAREHOLDER GULF

The evolution of the capital markets should in theory have levelled the playing field. We can be both employee and shareholder should we choose. But this does not appear to be what has happened in the case of most businesses. The gulf between owner and worker has, if anything, widened. Few of us fully understand the depth of the shareholder fixation. We are often unclear on the basic terms of valuation. We do not track the stock with any regularity. We only have a vague sense of what events impact the stock. This renders us out of touch and vulnerable. Most ideas emanating from board level management are articulated in terms of shareholder value. Unless we understand why, we rank amongst the masses of the excluded.

One critical law of survival is to move from thinking like an employee to thinking like an owner. Assuming the position of a shareholder is a powerful one. A small number of shares carries the same entitlement as a large number. With simply one solitary share you are empowered to vote, you can raise a debate at annual general meetings, you can object to corporate policy. Above all you can sell. In becoming a shareholder, you move from employment to stakeholdership.

Of course, you have to make the fact you follow the stock something that people know. Follow the indices, understand the analysts' estimates of performance, and understand what they consider drives performance. Frame conversations with your seniors in the context of the impact actions will have on share price. Always refer back to market capitalisation, PE's and earnings growth. This is the way the board thinks and it should also be the way you think. The more your actions are framed in terms of shareholder value, the more in tune you will be seen to be. Become a shareholder and you have a seat at the table of the workings of the CEO's mind. That is a table worth getting a reservation at.

The takeaway

Stock tracking is a simple business. From Yahoo Finance to Hoover-on-line, there are a welter of services that give you free daily information on stocks. If you own some, you will in all probability become hooked on watching its progress. If the firm for which you work is not quoted, then you can always find one or two public firms that compete in the same sector as your employer. Their share price performance will offer a great way to see how the market is viewing such firms, whether they are in or out of favour. Once plugged into the shareholder mindset, you will find that you react very differently to corporate events and the involuntary message you send will be the right one. *'I care about the stock'*. **Think, live, breathe share price.**

A TALE OF TWO DISMISSALS

They had listened to John Mowbray for perhaps fifteen minutes. Jo regretted she had ever asked the question in the first place. Joan Milroy rolled her eyes and exchanged a cautious smile with Jo. Jo had never expected to feel such an involuntary surge of empathy with Joan Milroy. It made the whole thing so much better.

'It's a quirk of accounting that's probably making it all look so bad. I don't know for sure but I would bet. We're having to write off three hundred million of computer amortisation in one year. Combine that with accelerated depreciation of goodwill from all the acquisitions and you have a serious dent to earnings. But that bears no relationship to real cash flow, of course.'

Jo had tried to follow him but it was pretty much unintelligible. She was just left with the impression that she was hopelessly out of her depth. If this was what it took to succeed at Communicopia, then she would be out of a job. Pronto.

'So that's probably why we're in this mess,' John Mowbray concluded with an ebullient rise in his voice. 'It's not cash flow. It's just accrual based earnings that are getting squeezed. It's not as serious as it looks.'

Joan Milroy smiled over at him laconically. 'Then, if nothing is really wrong, how come the share price has halved in a month?'

'You watch the shareprice?' he asked with a bemused smile.

'Of course. Don't you? As you yourself said, we're on a rating less than that of any competitor. That tells me something's very wrong.'

'Perhaps, but maybe the market's wrong as well.'

'I thought the market never gets it wrong?'

'I don't want to bore you with the theory, but if you knew finance you would know that's not always true.'

'So you're saying it doesn't matter that the firm's worth half what it was.'

'Well, yes. But in the long run . . .'

'You said it yourself. I doubt that's what Drinkwater's thinking. He owns five per cent of the company. We'd better ask him, eh?'

STEP 13. BREAK DEFENSIVE ROUTINES

The mindset of employment is one of obedience. Those that are disobedient and rebellious by nature often flunk out of school and become either entrepreneurs or social drop-outs. Society frequently admires the non-conformist but it tries to breed the dangerous quality out of us. Companies do exactly the same.

The problem with a mentality of obedience is that it can so easily lead to insecurity. Because we grow dependent on the relationship with our employer, we lose the confidence to hold independent views. The fruits of insecurity are what we call 'defensive routines'. When we are challenged from a position of insecurity we tend to defend ourselves as if we were under attack. Every criticism is taken as a personal assault. By defending the position we inevitably further entrench ourselves in it. Before long, we and that position become one and the same thing, until ultimately we have to defend it at all costs.

We are all guilty of defensive routines. We all harbour doubts about our abilities. We all feel vulnerable when our ideas are undermined. Faced with endless change initiatives, new management objectives and fragile job tenure, it is no wonder so many of us act defensively. If there is one obsession that stalks all management teams it is the need for continual change. Shareholders expect it and the rate of market development demands it. But continual change is not something any of us naturally feel comfortable with. We all crave predictability. When confronted with change we typically behave like any creature under attack. We seek to defend ourselves. Once a defensive routine is set in motion it is very hard to reverse. Positions become galvanised, viewpoints polarised. Confrontation becomes inevitable.

Often this cycle of defensiveness can be utterly unconscious, expressing itself in protestations of 'they just don't understand', 'I'm not appreciated', 'why don't they just get it?' It is a familiar pattern amongst those of us who suffer from insecurity – that we maintain strong opinions and points of view on issues even when, in our heart of hearts, we know we may not be right. This rigidity and reluctance to accept alternative viewpoints is tolerated at very senior levels of companies. But as a mere employee it leads to one inevitable outcome. Redundancy.

Breaking the cycle of defensiveness is central to your strategy of differentiation. Freeing yourself from defensive routines means that you can condition your stance, be flexible, roll with the blows. The non-defensive employee is likely to be perceived as highly adaptive and to be construed, rightly or wrongly, as a contributor. They are far more likely to endure. Employment in modern business is like living in a gale – you need to be flexible and supple. Defensiveness will eventually make you snap.

THE POWER OF FLEXIBILITY

The only viable route to achieve differentiation is to manage oneself out of defensive routines. There are some simple rules of thumb to achieve this:

a) demonstrate a balanced view by accepting the possibility of the existence of alternative perspectives.
b) encourage other people to express their position before you state yours. This buys you time to moderate your ideas in such a way as to avoid outright confrontation and assimilate elements of other people's thoughts into your own. As a colleague once warned me, *'Generally speaking, you aren't learning when your mouth is moving.'*
c) consult others to find out alternative views on a position before you mentally commit to it – consensual views are powerful views.
d) if possible, when expressing strong opinions always stick to facts rather than pure assertion or conjecture

The best summary of the state of mind this process gives rise to is openness. It is the same mental disposition that characterises a martial art such as Tai Chi. You use the weight and rigidity of others against them. Once you become conscious of this as a strategy, it will become violently obvious when other people are in the grip of defensive routines. As with many things in life, identifying the symptom is half the battle.

The takeaway

Defensive routines are like dry rot. You're not aware of them until your house falls down. But such a fate can be readily avoided. Use challenges to your assumptions and mental models to your advantage by assimilating alternative points of view and reworking them. The openness you exhibit will allow you to be seen as a promoter of change. We have explored four simple methods of conditioning your interaction with other people. Use them and you will **break defensive routines**.

A TALE OF TWO DISMISSALS

John Mowbray was smart. Jo had no doubt about that. But his reaction had left her wondering just how reliable his opinions actually were. Of course, there was no reason he should be interested in her point of view. As he said, she knew nothing about finance. But she suspected that all was not as calm inside John Mowbray as he would have them believe.

'Look, I don't mean to offend you, but what you're suggesting is simply crap' Jo responded, trying not to raise her voice.

'You mean you don't understand' he responded with a patronising smile.

'I asked you a simple question and all you give back is a riddle.'

'If you understood accounting you would know how wrong you are.'

'I don't think this is about accounting John. It's about you. You can't accept that maybe Joan is right.'

'Look Jo. Joan admitted it herself. She knows nothing about numbers. How can you say something like that and expect to be taken seriously?'

'I think John you're just using this accounting crap to hide the fact that you've no more idea than us why you're about to get fired.'

'Speak for yourself Jo. The problem with you is that you don't understand the first thing about how the business works, yet you're supposed to be promoting it to the outside world. That just doesn't add up. But then again I guess it's not so surprising, since you both admit you can't even add up in the first place.'

Jo was about to retaliate but she suddenly stopped herself and looked hard at John Mowbray. She was being stupid. It was obvious he was as nervous as she was, and now he was letting it show. That made them equals. It would just come down to simple odds. Nothing more.

Step 14. 'Screw you' cash

'If you think nobody knows you're alive,
try missing a couple of car payments.'

The greatest paranoia most of us face at work is, what happens if the salary checks stop coming? Could we survive for a month, three months, twelve months? The average mid-level employee earning between £15,000 and £40,000 typically has cash and cash equivalent reserves of no greater than a month of salary. That is not much buffer room. Out of a job and we are out of business.

In order to pursue a strategy of differentiation, we need confidence. We need sufficient self-conviction to sell our worth and capabilities to others. There is a simple rule of self-conviction – if you do not believe in yourself no one else is likely to. That is something we all learn early in life, typically in the playground. If you cannot defend your position for fear of being put at risk, your position will always be a weak one. At some point you have to generate the self-confidence to set your fears aside. But it is often a quality which adulthood breeds out of us. The sort of primal fear of the playground is replaced by something far more subtle – the fear that failure to tow the line will lead to rejection.

The predictability of employment also often deludes us into a false sense of security. The cheque arrives, it always will. As a consequence, we tend to raise our consumption habits to fill our earnings capability. There is a continual increase of personal expenditure in line with income. This phenomenon has no name but what it amounts to is 'employment inflation'. Because it occurs over the course of a long career, it is often hard to discern. It is a little like ageing. And, of course, the greater our credit card bill becomes, the weaker our ability to assert ourselves. Why does this matter? It matters because our degree of negotiating power with our employer is undermined.

Any job is nothing other than a continual exercise in negotiation. The only productive negotiation occurs between parties with similar perceived strength and a shared desire to achieve a positive outcome. Imbalanced negotiations, where the perceived power and respect of the parties is out of kilter, invariably wind up deteriorating into bitterness.

Mutual respect is not the usual hallmark of employer/employee relationships. Invariably the employer negotiates from a position of strength because they perceive they have their hands on the purse strings. In its negative manifestation, this is a license to exploitation. In most employment situations it is not that extreme. Indeed, there is no negotiation at all. Just passivity.

THE POWER OF THE UNDRAWN GUN

Our Five Forces model (Step 2) has shown us the danger of having one customer. As an employee there's not much you can do about having one customer. But you can erode the dependency. If you know that you can afford to resign when entering a negotiation with your boss, you act very differently. You will also be treated very differently. An employer needs to know that other options exist and that you should be valued accordingly. If you are perceived to have that manoeuvrability, the relationship will be much more like that between two businesses than between an individual on the one hand and an institution on the other. Reflect back on your five forces model again. Negotiating power over your one customer will be a key determinant of the quality of your working life. The tables will be balanced. This is why 'screw you' cash is at the core of all stable employment relationships.

The takeaway

Aim to accumulate liquid assets that are around six months of your annual income. They can be invested in bonds and blue chip stocks or other liquid instruments. This insurance policy will fundamentally alter the nature of your interaction with your employer. It may mean no new car every four years, no flat screen TV, no Sky Sport subscription, one less holiday on the Algarve, and putting up with that old, saggy sofa. But **'Screw you' cash** means you won't be ruled by the fear of being fired.

A TALE OF TWO DISMISSALS:

'I suppose the new generation simply have tastes beyond anything I could have imagined at your age.' Joan continued. 'We didn't even get a car until we were in our mid-thirties. It was unthinkable really. It's only since Peter retired that we've taken holidays abroad. Of course, things like that are much cheaper than they used to be.'

'I just can't imagine living without a new car', Jo laughed. 'Your thirties is the time to live life, to expand your horizons, not to clamp down on everything. I want to live, not huddle in dread that my pension may not be big enough.'

'Well, as I say, we're different generations I suppose. When you've seen your parents scrape into old age after the war, it's hard not to put a priority on saving. Always have, always will.'

'So how much have you saved then?'

Joan looked back at her abashed. 'That's quite an impertinent question Jo. I'd never dream of asking you that.'

'Come on Joan. I'm curious. Thirty thousand? Fifty thousand?' Jo stopped for a moment and looked for a change of expression on Joan's face. 'A hundred thousand?'

Joan had suddenly flushed red in a way Jo had never seen her do before.

'Joan. You're saying you've saved a hundred thousand and you still live in a flat out in Barking and drive an Austin Rover? Doesn't it ever strike you that may have been missing out on life?'

'No. If you really want to know it makes me feel good about myself. If it comes to it, I can do precisely what I like. Can you say the same Jo?'

Step 15. Family first

In the face of an ever more demanding work place, family is often viewed as a drain on attention better paid to lucrative employment. Why should dealing with kids' football matches and school reports distract us from our quarterly volume targets? How can we be expected to meet the mortgage payment, the car hire purchase payment, to pay for the holidays, if we don't focus one hundred per cent on the office? We are typically prepared to sacrifice family time for work but rarely the other way round. We have all become habituated to the idea that a successful career requires single-minded devotion. That is why we now on average defer having a family until our thirties. Business time is serious. Family time is frivolous.

In the self created war between home and work, work often decisively wins. That is where most energies are expended, that is where ambitions are realised. The price to be paid is divorce rates at fifty per cent but it appears this is a price many of us are prepared to pay.

The family brand

But there is also a price to be paid at work we are often unaware of. Our success outside work is a central element of our personal brand. It speaks volumes of our values, it gives us the strength to say no, it is the foundation of our personal equity. Pull that pillar away and the ceiling usually falls in shortly afterwards. Without this we lose our emotional balance. Our distance from the politics of work is negligible. We err towards defensive routines. Being prepared to change at work is hard to stomach if work is your whole life.

Most people choose to separate the two worlds of home and work. They do not involve their family in their place of labour. Their spouse is rarely seen. Colleagues and bosses know little of their home life. This has undoubtedly contributed to the shift of work from a relationship experience to one based on pure transactional qualities. The problem with transactional arrangements is that they are ultimately fickle. In choosing to accept this level of impersonality we also have to accept that we are more easily dispensable. We can be replaced without any emotion. We are not differentiated but hired and fired based on cost.

There is also a heavy toll to be paid in the home. If your family have no real idea what it is you do, if they have no sense of where you work, of your achievements and trusts, then they cannot possibly place a value on that aspect of your life. As a result, those you care about most care least about the bulk of your life's work.

The separation of home and work is not a successful strategy. A successful family life is one of the best assets in your strategic armoury. It is a wonderful reflection of independence from work. As work pervades ever more of our lives and companies become more demanding of ethical character, a sound family will become a prime barometer of individual ethics. If you are known to have a successful relationship you are more likely to be trusted. It will be adjudged that you can manage other people, that you are mature. Your negotiating position will be taken far more seriously.

If a firm understands something of your spouse, of your children, where you live, your aspirations, you are building an inclusive relationship that will create a more enduring contract between you and your employer. It is no different from building a relationship with a customer. To have a relationship the other party has to know something of you. All differentiation is based on relationships. At the end of the day, what else is there?

The takeaway

Uniting the two sides of your life will pay dividends. It is easily done. Put family photos on your desk and on your walls, of informal, relaxed, happy times together. Occasionally arrange to bring your kids in and show them round. Introduce them to colleagues. Involve your partner in firm gatherings. Find reasons to introduce him or her to your boss. Weave allusions to the joy of family into conversations. Importing that affection will lower barriers and bring you closer to the fabric of the company. As we will explore next, all businesses are no more than networks of relationships, which means they respond to social emotions more than anything else. Put **family first**.

A TALE OF TWO DISMISSALS

John Mowbray tried hard to disguise his contempt. Perhaps she had meant it to sound touching. But the way she phrased it, it just came across like a sad excuse for a non-career. The commercial world really didn't have room for that sort of sentiment. It was an embarrassment.

'So what did Drinkwater say? I'm amazed you had the guts to tell him.'

'He was nice about it really. He seemed to understand.' Joan answered with a frank smile.

'You told him the same way you just told me?'

'As you get older John you begin to understand these things are not embarrassing. They're real. Cancer's real.'

'Yes, but to tell him you had Ovarian cancer and would have to have a hysterectomy. That's probably a level of detail he didn't need.'

'Maybe so. But I wanted him to realise I wasn't just reducing my hours for no reason. It was only six months. That was two years ago. It hasn't affected my contribution.'

'I don't think I've ever brought any aspect of my home life to work. It seems inappropriate, unprofessional.'

'Perhaps you don't have a home life John?' Jo interrupted sharply.

'It's true, work takes up most of my energy. But I see that as good. What relevance is it to anyone whether I have no kids or five? Look at you Jo. We all know you took the full maternity leave on offer. Don't tell me that's not one of the reasons you're sitting here now?'

Jo didn't respond.

'I don't think he minded.' Joan continued musingly. 'In fact I think he was probably glad to help.'

'Drinkwater helped? You mean he didn't reprimand you?' John Mowbray asked with a look of amazement.

'No, actually he got the company to cover the cost of a private bed. He said it was an embarrassment that the insurance didn't cover spouses.'

John Mowbray looked at her blankly, wondering if she were somehow winding him up.

Step 16. Politics Matter

So far it has all been pretty clean and above board. Strategy always has that clinical quality. Strategy provides a set of plans, of rules. But winning the battle requires engagement and engagement is never strategic. It is bloody, it is tactical, it is improvised and opportunistic. You have to get your hands dirty.

The competitive tactics managers use to rule companies are called politics. Of course, the euphemism often used for corporate politics is management. You can take courses in management, there are even degrees in the 'science' of management. But whatever nice labels we give it, it is politics that gets things done.

Politics has a dirty name. We deride work environments which are excessively political. We berate firms which promote people based on politics not performance. We are suspicious of individuals with an obsessive concern to win the patronage of those in power. But, like it or not, no large social group can operate without a political process. What we call management is in fact largely politics – a subtle process of negotiation and persuasion necessary to get key people to support an action or decision.

Contrary to popular perception, politics is also a

highly democratic process. The more politics in a system, the more democratic the management process will be. The voices will be more distinct and more debate will be tolerated. Politics can only be quashed by dictatorship. Bad management is usually nothing more than dictatorship dressed up. So you shouldn't feel bad about honing your political skills. The political process is about understanding the social currents of the organisation, positioning yourself well to harness them and aligning yourself with the right people. People who are successful at differentiating themselves also tend to be good politicians.

THE RELATIONSHIP GAME

The object of the political process in an organisation is to develop relationships. Without relationships nothing gets done, whether it be changing work methods, approving a budget or getting the go-ahead to give a customer a discount. Relationships, and the trust that exists in good relationships, are the DNA of decision making.

We tend to have a limited interpretation of what constitutes a relationship. In our common definition it usually involves some level of intimacy, perhaps love, and it is not a bond we think of as relevant to the work place. In fact there are many types of relationship, ranging from the purely transactional to the profoundly emotional. Transactional relationships are those that oil the wheels of trade. It is easier to sell a consulting project to a client with whom you have a longstanding rapport. It is easier to persuade a fellow employee to adopt a new method of working if some history of trust has been established. The antithesis of this is the cold call. Cold calling doesn't just occur down a telephone. It occurs when you try to get things done with the help of people with whom you have no relationship. It doesn't work very well. Without relationships you can't function and without relationships you won't matter. If you don't care and no one cares about you, then you are easy road kill.

Given this, it is extraordinary how little attention most of us dedicate to building webs of relationships at our place of work. Sure, we might have some friendships, we might have some laughs on Friday afternoon. We might even have some love affairs. But that is not a political strategy. A political strategy means building a web of relationships with as wide a constituency as possible. Clearly, these relationships will differ both in type and intensity, and we cannot afford to stretch ourselves too thin. But the impact we have on an organisation, and therefore our level of security, are not best measured in terms of our efficiency alone, but in terms of the strength of relationships we have built up. That is, after all, all businesses are – bundles of relationships.

RELATIONSHIP MAPPING

The inconvenient thing about relationships is that they cannot be weighed up or measured – *'My relationship with Paul has shifted from five to three on the Richter scale this week, oh dear.'* It is perhaps for that reason that we forget how valuable they are.

Despite this, you *can* monitor the strength of your political network. The most effective way to do this is to refer back to your value chain, and in each segment of it write down the names of the people that matter to you in your daily life. What will become apparent is where in the organisation your relationship base is strong and where it is weak and needs strengthening. This will alert you to where you must invest energy building up better relationships. You should also ask yourself how well they are distributed between bosses, peers and subordinates. Again, it would be unwise to assume all that matters are bosses. Without the affection of peers and the loyalty of subordinates, your ship will ultimately get wrecked on the rocks of change. Nor should your relationships be limited to the company itself. Your web of connections should extend to customers, to suppliers, to trade bodies, and to journalists.

The resulting map of relationships will be the most accurate and relevant description of what your place of work means to you. It is not buildings, machines, product lines or bank accounts. It is people. Sounds pretty simple, but is that really how you chart your work now? Admit it. Probably not. It is the growth, and management of your relationship network that will determine the stability of your working life. You can either master these political skills or be subject to a political process in which you have no voice.

The takeaway

Put aside whatever it is you use to idle away your evenings in front of the TV – reading the football scores, knitting that scarf, reading John Grisham. Instead, build up a relationship map. Review where it stands once a week, where the gaps lie, and where you have failed to invest energy. Put it up on the wall and enjoy the pleasure of watching it slowly fill out and expand. It is as much a conquest as when Vasco de Gama drew his impressions of the world he was sailing across on his epic voyages of discovery. Remember, **politics matter**.

A TALE OF TWO DISMISSALS

'What I don't get Joan, is how you can seriously claim to have a relationship with Drinkwater. Are you sure you're not deluding yourself a little?' Jo laughed.

She couldn't help herself. Something about Joan was both beguiling but also hopelessly naive. Jo had come to the conclusion that perhaps the past hour hadn't been wasted after all. She was learning just how self-deceiving people could be at Communicopia. It was clear to her that Drinkwater was just in this to make money for himself. Yet somehow he had managed to cultivate the kind of misguided loyalty shown by Joan, even amongst the most inconsequential of people. The reality was no one had proper relationships with each other at a company like Communicopia. There was no time for it.

'I didn't know you were a sycophant Joan. You seem too, well, too lacking in diplomacy for that.'

'What does sycophant mean Jo? You're beyond me.'

'Sliming up. Ass kissing. You know.'

'You'd better ask John about that.'

John Mowbray gave a fake smile and turned to Jo. 'If she doesn't know what sycophant means, that doesn't exactly suggest she's very good at being one, does it?'

Joan remained silent for a while before responding.

'Jo, I don't understand why everything you say is a sort of challenge. I hope you don't see me as some sort of threat do you?'

Jo didn't respond but smiled ironically.

'Good,' Joan continued. 'What matters to me is that I have a good relationship with the people I like. I don't get paid a lot, so there has to be something to get me in here every morning. Other people is all I've got.'

'Including Drinkwater?'

'Yes, including John Drinkwater. And why not?'

'Because right now he's the enemy.'

'That's where we differ Jo.'

'I think that's the one thing uniting the three of us actually. We have a common adversary for once.'

STEP 17. HOG KNOWLEDGE

Information has always meant power. The more widely sourced, the more timely and the better information you possess, the more power you will have. What distinguishes the CEO from line managers and equally gifted employees is that they control a far broader, more timely and more accurate spectrum of information – on customer spending patterns, on employee productivity, on bottom line performance. This information is one of the keys to their success.

It is in the nature of all institutions to be paranoid about defending the privacy of information. Since it is information that gives leaders their power, this is hardly surprising. Rather than relying on employing talented, knowledgeable people, there has been a concerted push to transform personal knowledge into company data that can be protected. The IT boom of the past fifteen years has seen an increasing move to institutionalising information and knowledge. The objective is simple – to take the tacit knowledge that exists around an organisation, codify it, organise it and render it institutional property. It assumes that what is essentially a personal asset can be turned impersonal, and added to the balance sheet of the firm. This process is called 'knowledge management'.

This represents a real threat to the stability of employment. Traditionally, highly rewarded employment has been based on expertise. The more skilled an individual becomes in a particular task, the less dispensable they become and the higher salary they command. Knowledge management promises the firm the ability to break that bond of personalisation. If employees are no longer experts, then they are also dispensable and can be paid less.

OF BOTTLENECKS AND KNOWLEDGE

An employee that is deemed to be immensely knowledgeable is likely to become a knowledge guardian. Being known as a knowledge guardian is a highly differentiated and defensible position. Knowledge guardians are rarely fired. The key is to become the point of reference for certain more complex or subjective forms of information, which are central to daily decision making.

The acid test of attaining knowledge guardianship is whether other people need the information you control to perform their job. That is to say, to what degree can you act as an information bottleneck. Bottlenecks may be the bête noire of management, but they are inevitable. Someone has to be the knowledge-holder. You should reflect back on your Five Forces. Were you to be removed, what would the consequences be? Would the system falter, would client contracts go unfulfilled? Would key lieutenants lack the know-how to pick up the ball?

When you began your career you would not perhaps have ever envisaged yourself becoming a knowledge guardian (even if it does sound a little like a Jedi knight). But in the search for personal differentiation it is a sobriquet you should strive for. Knowledge is one of the hardest things to substitute and one of the most expensive things for a firm to develop. It is a major driver of the 'goodwill' that makes up (on average) sixty per cent of the value of any company. Pick your areas of tacit knowledge, cultivate them and defend them.

The takeaway

Return to your value drivers. There will be some where you have knowledge that is crucial to the efficient functioning of a key part of the firm. Understand what it is about your knowledge of the situation that is unique. Ensure that others understand its significance to the firm and share your particular appreciation of it. Once you have found a bottleneck all of your own, you would be well advised to guard it carefully. Go on, **hog knowledge**.

'But Jo, a moment ago you and John were calling me stupid. If I'm stupid why would anyone care what I think?' Joan said in an injured tone.

'Joan, you know what, I don't really know,' Jo replied softly. 'But if you didn't matter I assume we wouldn't be sitting in this room together. Secretaries usually get fired with a telephone call. They don't get an interview. That's the preserve of executives.'

'Well I'll tell you Jo, I'll let you into a little secret.'

'You have a secret? I thought that wasn't allowed,' Jo replied sarcastically.

'There's one thing I've got which no one else has.'

'Don't tell me. Dirty photos of Drinkwater?'

'I'm serious Jo. I know you don't think I've got anything to offer but . . .'

'I was only joking Joan. I know you've lots to offer and I never meant to suggest you were stupid. So what's the secret?'

'I've kept track of everyone's birthdays. I'm the only one who knows how old everyone is at headquarters.'

'Well, that's fantastic. But I don't get what good that would do anyone.'

'You got a birthday card last year from Drinkwater didn't you?'

'Yes, it's true. I was surprised.'

'It's his pet thing.' Joan said in a quieter voice.

'Well, that's pretty weird for a CEO.'

'How's he going to do it without the list?' Joan continued.

'He's going to fire us all and start again. That'll just about solve it don't you think?' Jo laughed.

'Jo. Sometimes I really believe you're as cynical as you make out.'

Step 18. Be client-facing at all times

There is a basic division at the core of most companies – the marketers versus the managers. The managers look inwards and the marketers look outwards. Like something from a Greek myth, modern business is a beast with eyes on two sides of its head. But it is the managers that usually dictate the nature of our work lives.

Managers have been increasingly adopting a process view of their firms – that the company is not a collection of specialist functions but a set of linked processes. The pressure on the employee in a process conscious environment is to conform to the rules and master the processes. You are required to become outstanding at processing the maximum number of claims forms per day or dealing with the maximum number of customer enquiries. Your efficiency may even be monitored by a computer. There is only one sure outcome of such an impetus – that the process will become larger than you or I, the individual. It is a slippery slope for us to head down.

The process view makes one big assumption. That there is automatically work to be done. But all machines need to be fed. Bringing in clients and contracts is the one thing no firm can do without. The only people who remain resolutely larger than the process are those that feed it. The only people who ultimately can't be cut are those that bring in revenue. In the battle of manager versus marketer, the latter is the party with which to align yourself. Having client relationships is as good a guarantee of security as you can reasonably get.

BACK TO RELATIONSHIP MATTERS

The focus here is on client relationships, not simply sales. The world is full of salesmen but good client relationship managers are rare.

It is a myth put about by consultants and bankers that firms are impersonal collections of processes and assets. Firms are nothing more than bundles of relationships – relationships with suppliers, with the trade, with end-customers. This idea is intensely unsettling for financial markets and intermediaries. Relationships seem too ephemeral, and too tacit. But the reality is that all firms that successfully differentiate their products or services are customer-relationship based. At the other end of every transaction is an individual, not an organisation. The manager or employee who focuses on cultivating relationships may prove the best selling weapon the firm has, even if their employer won't dare admit it to themselves.

In a client dominated world what matters is relationships. Too few of them and of the wrong sort and you are dispensable. Many and of the right sort and you are irreplaceable. Strong commercial relationships often take a long time to build. They can also be cultivated with many different people within a client organisation. The key is to be able to distinguish between those relationships that matter and those that do not.

HAVING A PRICE ON YOUR HEAD

The best employment security one can possibly achieve is the certainty that if you walk the client walks too. However, even if you do not have this sort of role, you can always refer back what you do to the customer experience. Among the value drivers you have identified, you need to try and ensure that at least half can be directly traced through to the customer experience. Above all, you have to exercise great caution when it comes to moving from client interface (the external face of the company), to line management (the internal face of the company). There will be inducements to do so – a big title, prestige, a larger office. But accepting the inducements unhesitatingly carries its risks. If you have client revenue to your name you have a clear and obvious value.

The takeaway

Have a keen understanding of how you drive client value. If possible, retain direct client relationships. It is better to have a small number of intense client relationships than a large number of customer 'situations'. Relationships, not sales, are what matter. Ensure these relationships are personalised, not institutionalised. That is your ticket to ride – forever. **Be client-facing at all times**.

A TALE OF TWO DISMISSALS

'You and I are not so very different' Joan Milroy responded after a long, tense pause.

John Mowbray looked over at her dismissively.

'You can look at me like that, but you know what I mean,' Joan continued.

'Joan, I have absolutely no idea what you mean at all. You're going to have to enlighten me.'

'We're both seen as overhead. That's what unites us John. You may be twenty years younger than me. You may have gone to university, to some la-di-da private school. You may know how to read a financial statement, how to make Drinkwater take what you say seriously. But really John, you and I are not so different.'

'I don't understand. It sounds like you're ranting.'

'When did you last win a client for the company? Could you really claim you've brought in even a penny of revenue in your three years here?'

'That's not my job. I'm not a salesman.'

'You mean you're above that?'

'I didn't spend two years at business school to sell media space Joan. I'm a manager. Don't be obtuse about it.'

'That's right John. I'm dense. I'm dense to have let myself become an overhead. I guess you were born to it. But I had a choice. I made a bad choice getting lumped with the likes of you.'

Step 19. Keep to the core

The focus of corporate activity over the past five years has been on cutting away non core activities. The capital markets have increasingly favoured firms that stick firmly to their core competencies. As a result the vast, lumbering behemoths, from British Airways to Hanson Industries to BT, have all sold off or closed down the pieces of their groups which were not strictly in their heartland.

If there is one place you don't want to be, it is employed in part of the company that is not considered core. There is only one fate for a non-core asset. Assuming it is not a total dog, it will be broken off and sold. Keep in mind that any change of control resulting from a sale creates intense employment risk. The acquirer will almost certainly look to reduce operating costs to justify their purchase. That is the way of all deals.

Knowing core from non-core

Sometimes the firm will be quite clear about what constitutes its core business. It is likely to comprise the bulk of its revenues, to contribute the bulk of its profits and to be the area in which the firm has specialised for years – all pieces of information it will disclose on its website or in its annual report.

But often it is surprisingly hard to know whether you are working in the core or on the periphery. This is not so surprising if you consider that senior management will periodically alter their own views as to what is core and what is not. You have to hone your skills at identifying the give-away signs that such a change of view is afoot.

The usual prelude to getting rid of non-core parts of a business is a consulting project. As soon as the consultants appear it is a fairly safe bet that a question mark exists in the mind of management whether a unit should be sold or closed down. The appearance of consultants can often be misleadingly exciting. Getting drawn into working with the consultants on their projects is a very seductive proposition. The pace of the work is faster, you have an opportunity to view the business objectively, the exposure is 'sexy'. The consultants themselves, often young, with no experience of operating a business, find it hard to move beyond theory. They therefore need capable people to champion the cause within the organisation. But as an insider such a role is an Indian summer: it is doomed to end. When the project ends the consultants go. If you become dedicated to their project, at the end you will probably have nowhere to go other than down with the non-core asset.

The other classic sign of a potentially non-core asset is that it will be more exciting than the dull, staple of the old core. Core businesses tend by definition to be mature and slower growth. The career process will be rigid and well defined, progress slow moving. Non-core businesses, by contrast, tend to be less formalised, faster paced and as a result appear to offer more opportunity.

In buoyant times firms are always tempted to dabble in fast, sexy new ventures. The Internet has been the most spectacular example in recent history. Mature, otherwise sensible firms, lavished vast fortunes on hair-brained web ventures. Good people are encouraged to try their hand, with all the gung-ho-ness of explorers setting off to discover new territories. If you strike gold, fine. But, in all probability, there will come a time when such activities are recognised for what they are – bunny trails. And particularly so if, like so many ventures of this sort, they consume vast amounts of money. Should times get tougher for the parent, then look out below.

The takeaway

Core businesses tend to be at the dull end of the spectrum. By definition, they are mature and lower growth areas which means less excitement and, in some ways, less opportunity. But, by the same token, they also tend to be less competitive internally and offer more opportunities for personal differentiation against relatively uninspired competition. **Keep to the core,** not the periphery.

A TALE OF TWO DISMISSALS

'What I don't get Joan, is you've been around long enough to know better,' Jo said musingly. 'John and I are new kids on the block. How long is it now? Twelve years?'

'Thirteen actually.' Joan responded with a bashful smile.

'Thirteen years and you're still sitting in the same old bit of the business. If I'd had the chance I would have moved to the on-line publishing group the first opportunity I'd had. Everyone knows the future's in paperless copy. That's where all the advertising's going to be. I bet no one's going to get fired from the on-line group. Unfortunately I arrived too late to make the switch. But you on the other hand Joan, you had every opportunity to do so.'

'Why should I have?' Joan responded with a bemused look. 'It happens every few years – some hysteria about the latest thing. I've seen it a few times over the last ten years. One minute it's the greatest thing since sliced bread, the next it's old hat. I prefer to stick to the business I know. When I hear my grandson talking about it, then maybe I'd think differently. He hasn't said anything about looking at on-line ads; not a peep. Personally, I don't see it at all. But perhaps that's just old-fashioned me.'

'That's the problem at Communicopia, you know Joan. We haven't moved with the times. There's too much inertia. I would bet that's why were in the mess we are. Management has done nothing to force people to change with the technology. We're dinosaurs.'

Step 20. Grasp nettles

How did the big bosses get big? It is a question we all inevitably ask ourselves when we look up at some of the people running the show. How on earth did she manage to get there? Is she really so different from me? How can she possibly justify pulling in half a million when I get twenty grand and do all the work?

There is one characteristic that will tend to unite all the top-dogs and fat-cats. More often than not, at some point in their professional lives they will have pulled off a turnaround. There is no surer way to establish a reputation than salvaging a basket case. People always admire saviours, and shareholders are no different.

It requires an unusual resolve to turn a problem business around. Such a situation represents a sizeable personal risk. It is far easier to enjoy association with something that is already successful. That is why the hot graduates flock in droves to Goldman Sachs and McKinsey. We are all fundamentally risk averse. But there is, of course, a precise correlation between risk and reward. The potential rewards for grasping an unattractive problem are always far greater than the rewards of avoiding risk altogether. It just depends on our appetite.

All firms have their monsters and problem children; the disasters they would prefer to forget all about in the hope they will simply go away. In an age of employee insecurity most people naturally want to distance themselves from the company cock-ups – the failing business line, the unprofitable division, the malfunctioning process. We, as self-preserving people, are understandably nervous about shouldering accountability. The result is that most firms are littered with problems with no obvious owners. No one wants to grasp the nettle.

OF NETTLE GRASPERS

One way to build a fearsome reputation in a company is to be known as a nettle grasper, someone who is willing to take on the problem, to find solutions to messes created by other people. It is like mine-clearing. Not glamorous, but universally admired. But who actually wants to do it? The reality is, provided you didn't create the problem in the first place, the risks of taking a problem child under your wing are lower than you might expect. Should you fail, you are likely to get a consolatory pat on the back. But your efforts will be appreciated. Should you succeed, then you are truly on the path to differentiation.

This is precisely the route taken by many high profile CEOs who have risen from the ranks. Your own travails do not have to be as epic in proportions. Problematic product lines, faulty production processes, unproductive marketing efforts, malfunctioning distribution systems, inefficient word processing methods – all are legitimate targets. Nor does it necessarily mean rolling up your sleeves. Often, a few well-aimed ideas for what can be done will be enough to identify yourself as a problem solver.

By being a nettle grasper, it is possible to temporarily assume a role that is far senior to the position you would normally occupy. It is likely there will be little hierarchy to deal with and a minimal approval process. It is also an opportunity to apply your ingenuity, your common sense, unfettered by company protocol. That means more personal profile and the opportunity to differentiate. Seize it.

The takeaway

Every problem you can find represents an opportunity to distinguish yourself. It may sound paradoxical, (surely it is better to stick with activities that present no risk). But as long as problems do not originate from you, solving them carries remarkably little risk. And what risk there is, is typically worth taking. **Grasp nettles**.

A TALE OF TWO DISMISSALS

'That sounds utterly perverse logic to me' Joan Milroy finally snapped. 'I can't believe you could be so callous.'

'Look, Joan, if he's prepared to get rid of executives at the centre then he must know something we don't. It must be pretty bad. I don't know about you, but I'd prefer to get out before the thing goes down, if it's going down. I've got my track record to think about. No one employs someone in finance when they've been part of a bankruptcy.'

'So you'll actually be glad if he fires you?'

'Well, if things are on the brink, maybe it'd be a blessing in disguise. What's so very strange about that?'

'It just seems a sorry way to lead your life – running scared.'

'It's not running scared Joan. It's being pragmatic. You think Drinkwater gives a shit about our feelings, about our commitment? No, of course not.'

'Perhaps he would care if he thought you could help him?'

'Be serious Joan. How can we really help him? He's brought the company here. The question is, can he get it out of the hole he's dug.'

'So you don't want to get your hands dirty then?'

'It's not a question of getting my hands dirty. It's a question of being a sacrificial lamb.'

Jo Parker laughed out loud. 'We're already sacrificial lambs John. The question is, will we be barbecued or fried?'

STEP 21. GORGE ON TRAINING

All advanced societies take training very seriously. The act of being educated shapes our entire concept of what it means to be part of a society. Our first twenty years of life are largely dedicated to it, along with around ten per cent of our country's GDP.

Given this, it is surely bizarre that the moment you step across the threshold of the average employer, all formal education ostensibly comes to an end. This is always strenuously denied of course. Any senior executive asked will avow, hand on heart, a commitment to training. However, practically speaking, it is seen as a distraction from productive work. It is easier for firms to hire trained people than to accept the logic of carrying out the training themselves. As a result, they spend up to ten per cent of revenues promoting their brands and less than one per cent training and educating the very people who make their brands live. The reason is simple: cash spent on training hits the bottom line immediately, but the benefits are slow to feed through. If a skilled person is hired, the immediate cost is offset by an immediate benefit.

Sadly this logic ignores the one lesson history has indisputably taught us which is that the only sure way to succeed as a society is to prioritise education. Firms are just mini-societies. It is also important for individuals to understand this. Learning more makes us more marketable. It flows directly to our personal balance sheet and will undoubtedly advance our march through the life of work.

CAPITALISING ON PARADOXES

Although employers can discourage training or be unenthusiastic about initiating it, they value the result. Once your employer has invested heavily in training you, you move from being a cost to being an asset. The logic of letting such an asset go becomes less compelling. Firms will sometimes train in return for commitment. The consulting firms pioneered this when they started sponsoring employees through business schools. The more a firm invests in you, the more you will feel like an asset rather than a contracted employee. Firms naturally are more comfortable with asset mentality. It comes from a long history of balance sheet finance. They only very reluctantly write assets off.

Company-sponsored training may also offer you the chance to see beyond the palisade of your employer. It will give you skills that are relevant to the entire industry. It will offer you insights into the strategies of other firms and industry-wide practice. Instead of focusing solely on your position within your firm, you can also keep an eye on the broader industry. If you are assiduous in assimilating the bigger picture and honing general skills, you will be marketable well beyond the confines of your particular job.

Every minute you spend improving your knowledge

will enrich your personal equity. It may cost you in the short-term – in time, in money, in advancement. It may mean that for a while you cannot take out the jumbo mortgage or upgrade to the bigger car. But every dollar, pound or euro ploughed into education will yield a far higher return than any investment Warren Buffett has ever cooked up. Its payback in the longer term will be absolute.

The takeaway

Take every opportunity you get to learn, whether functional skills, industry standards or merely trade association gossip. Every grain of professional learning is another brick in your personal equity. Get enough bricks and the firm will lose too much to ever contemplate knocking you down. **Gorge on training**.

A TALE OF TWO DISMISSALS

'That's what you're really sore about isn't it Joan,' John Mowbray continued. 'The fact is you've got a chip on your shoulder. You look at people like me, like Jo. We're the product of privilege. We've been to college, got our further degrees. That gives us something you can never have.'

'That's cruel John.' Joan replied sullenly.

'I didn't mean it to sound cruel. It's just the truth.'

'You think you've got a monopoly on learning do you?'

'I didn't say that.'

'But you are saying the fact that I've spent the last three years working towards my business diploma means nothing. All those evenings I've put in were a waste?'

'I just don't see what it can really add. You're paid to be an administrator, not to learn about business plans. Perhaps the fact you've spent two weeks every year going on courses is why you're in this room now? Did you ever think of it that way?'

'I don't believe that's got anything to do with it actually. Besides, if I do get laid off, it's going to make it a lot easier to get another job.'

'I don't see the connection frankly.'

'That's because you take it for granted.'

'Joan, it's that chip again.'

'Besides, if you're so well educated, how come you didn't spot this coming months ago. Answer that one, Mr. Smarty Pants.'

Step 22. Get patronised

As Shakespeare wrote, '*some are born great . . . some achieve greatness . . . and some have greatness thrust upon them*'. What he did not mention was a single characteristic that unites all three. All the great people we remember from the fabric of the history of humanity had sponsors. Everyone needs a leg up. Someone has always occupied the seat you are sitting in, and the seat you aspire to sit in will almost certainly be currently occupied. For you to progress, someone somewhere has to be able to envisage you occupying that chair. That person is called a patron.

We no longer think in terms of patrons. It is a term associated with Renaissance artists and Florentine princes. The management stage is populated with bosses. It is with these individuals that we invest most of our energy. But that alone is not sufficient. We also need to find allies who look at us with more magnanimity and whose purpose is served by seeing us secure and rising. Such people are patrons. In order to secure one's position and climb the ladder, everyone needs someone to support them.

Picking the right sponsor is probably one of the toughest and most significant professional decisions you will make in a firm. It cannot be the boss. It is probably someone who has been in the organisation a while, and seen the comings and goings of a generation of employees. They will usually not dominate but have a more advisory, avuncular role. They may be retired managers or perhaps consultants or advisors. They may be people approaching retirement who no longer feel the competitive spirit.

Firms are bad at harnessing older people. The brave new world of commerce is seen as a young person's game. The result is that there are often a number of wise old birds sitting around organisations, too established to fire but ostensibly robbed of power. They make perfect sponsors. They know the politics. They have a rich store of knowledge and personal stratagems. Above all, they have motive. Their only hope of posterity is helping others to rise in their image.

THE POLITICS OF FLATTERY

So how do you win over a patron and manage a relationship like no other you will have in the organisation? The answer is simple. Promote your cause by making your patron feel good about him or herself. It is the oldest, most trusted technique in the book.

Flattery has acquired an immensely negative connotation in recent times. In that Shakespearean phrase, it is something 'vile politicians' engage in. Divisive and misguided flattery does indeed come across as odious stupidity. But well placed flattery serves a legitimate role. Like all marketing activity, it has to be targeted and refined. Sponsors have to be thought of as internal clients that will in turn pay you back with services in kind. What is it that makes them passionate? How do they like to be communicated with? How frequently? The best way to win a loyal sponsor is to boost their ego. A well-aimed strategy of sincere flattery will achieve precisely that.

The takeaway

Once you have won yourself a sponsor, it is likely that your level of security in the shifting political sands of employment will be much more secure. Sponsors are like insurance policies. A whisper in the right ear and you are differentiated from the mob. In a redundancy situation it can make all the difference. **Get patronised.**

A TALE OF TWO DISMISSALS

Jo had been pacing round the room. It had been almost an hour. What the hell did Drinkwater think he was playing at, keeping them penned-up like this? She would have to make it back by six-thirty or the au pair would be champing at the bit. Staring out at the Thames for too long was becoming dangerously depressing. It was not a sentiment she could afford to let get a grip of her right now. She had to be strong. For Joanne's sake if not for her own.

The strangest thing was Drinkwater was probably no more than twenty feet away from where she was standing. She wondered what thoughts were going through his mind. Whether she figured at all in them. She doubted it. If he wanted to get rid of them he should just have done it, rather than torment them like this. He would probably not be alone. There would be a committee of some sort. Perhaps some senior VPs or division heads. Who knows. The fact was, she had no idea who might be there. It was embarrassing really now she thought about it. She had got to know virtually nobody outside her publicity department in two whole years. She didn't have time, and now even less so with Joanne to contend with.

In the department they joked about the grey haired phantoms, the men from the corporate department who came by from time to time to get some information for an article in some obscure publication or other. They were demanding and frankly irritating. One or two of them would probably be there. Perhaps it would be one of the old farts who would actually pull the trigger. Drinkwater probably didn't want his fingerprints on the gun after all.

Step 23. Be curious

As humans we have curiosity hardwired into us. Allegedly, experiments have shown that primates are more motivated to find out what is on the other side of a closed door than by the prospect of food or even sex. From Scott of the Antarctic to Madame Curie, countless talented people have laid down their lives in the pursuit of discovery. We all lust to know the reasons why things are the way they are.

Given this naturally curious predisposition, it is extraordinary how most of us manage to suppress it in our place of work. Most of our energies are expended in mastering predefined processes, and conforming to corporate standards. We rarely question the system in which we work or encourage others to think outside the box. The box is us.

There is a good reason for our apparent dumbness. Firms are not set up to accommodate internal debate. They are not typically tolerant of critical enquiry. From time to time a fad for employee consultation bursts onto the scene but, in most firms, it is left to outsiders to ask the tough questions.

The presence of non-executive directors on the board is intended to act as an independent balance at the heart of the organisation. But usually the tough inquisition only comes from institutional investors and their analysts. '*Why is the share price falling? What is happening to costs? Why is executive pay spiralling? Why has the firm embarked on a rash of acquisitions*?' The fact that these questions are only asked by outsiders suggests that the governance process is flawed. Productive self-questioning has, by definition, to come from inside. We have to find the answers ourselves, even if we do need expert guidance on the way.

DID CURIOSITY REALLY KILL THE CAT?

Of course, it is easy to see the benefit to the firm of sparking internal debate about better ways of doing things. But what possible good can it do you and I? Joining the ranks of the agents provocateurs sounds like a recipe for disaster.

In fact, asking the tough questions identifies you with the process of change rather than stasis, and marks you out as someone who is prepared to tackle the tough issues in order to move the company on. But most of us are more comfortable answering than asking. We are naturally on the defensive. Asking searching questions can be embarrassingly misconstrued as offensive and intrusive. Tact is often a more powerful impulse than curiosity. But questioning need not be such a negative process, provided it does not undermine the person or custom being questioned and prods the person involved to find new answers themselves.

This was precisely the method promulgated by Socrates in first century Athens. By forcing pupils to question their assumptions, he inspired them to learn for themselves. This sort of questioning is far from offensive. It is reinforcing. A question is asked which challenges an assumption, but also invites an answer with which both parties can ultimately agree. The inquiry makes the respondent feel good about finding a new answer for themselves. Such a process cannot be confrontational. It has to be aimed at finding grounds for new resolution. *'I hadn't seen things that way, but now I can see that maybe . . .'*

Mastering the process of questioning the status quo in a mutually reinforcing manner will make you an agent of change but also an agent of resolution. It means you are never foisting your particular viewpoint on anyone else. But nor are you succumbing to passivity. Ask your manager, *'Have you thought . . . ?'*, ask a colleague *'What about . . . ?'* For every question demanded of you, ask one in return. Inevitably, the Socratic master becomes a teacher.

The takeaway

All too often, enquiry is seen as confrontation. Given the instability of work we are all understandably on the defensive. But it need not be this way. Positive, reinforcing enquiry is a great force for change. You may feel bashful or awkward about it, but by asking, you will unlock the enthusiasms of others. It is a moral endeavour that can only result in good. **Be curious.**

A TALE OF TWO DISMISSALS

Jo was sick of listening to Joan and John. It had been almost an hour and a half sitting in this small, airless room, without even so much as a glass of water. Perhaps Drinkwater was a big shot, but it didn't say much of the value he placed on them that he should leave them waiting like this. But perhaps that was the point. He wanted to make sure they understood just where they stood – nowhere.

Suddenly she became aware that Joan Milroy had been examining her with a contemplative, but fixed look.

'I think even if he doesn't fire you, you've decided to leave. Isn't that so?' she said without reacting to Jo's irritated glance.

'I don't know what I want at this point. Do any of us? I just want to get out of here I guess.'

'Perhaps you should look at it differently?' Joan added softly.

'What do you mean?'

'This is a chance for you to decide whether you really want to be here.'

'And if I do?'

'Then defend yourself. Argue why it makes sense to have you around. Explain what you've done so far, what more you can do.'

'You mean as if this were some sort of job interview or something?'

'Exactly.' Joan answered with a gentle smile of gratification.

Step 24. Train Disciples

Every great religious leader, from Jesus to Krishna, had disciples, and for a reason. Accumulating a following is the only way to ensure one's message is heard and propagated effectively. Unless others believe your ideas and voice them, these ideas are nothing. This is why we all need disciples. Disciples endorse our message, they defend our ideas, they preserve our position.

But that is not the way most of us think. We live in an age of intense individualism. We tend to view ourselves as one-person fortresses, from which we compete alone for selfish rewards. Modern management has reinforced this ethic. The focus on personal performance evaluation has ensured the demise of collective responsibility. Outsourcing, which places a preference on hiring freelancers, has simply accelerated this trend. We compete alone.

The result of such a fragmented, competitive existence is that we all inevitably look upwards. What matters is what our boss thinks of us, how we are evaluated, how we each perform as individuals. We long for the recognition of senior people we rarely ever meet. Any small glance is interpreted as promising glory or dismissal. We live perpetually on edge. Such solitariness breeds insecurity. It is not a satisfying existence.

LOOK DOWN AS WELL AS UP

Things need not be that way. We have talked about upward marketing (Step 10), but equally important is building a power-base amongst those below you. It is they who can carry you upwards. Looking down is perhaps more important than looking up. Bosses change and so do political power bases. Disciples move more slowly. Nothing is more powerful than popular endorsement.

It takes a peculiar skill to inspire the admiration of those who are less experienced than you. Part of it is feeding aspiration – being someone who other people want to emulate, because of skills, decency and diplomacy. Part of it is warmth, compassion and patience – the willingness to understand concerns and provide guidance that enables inexperienced people to work through to a personal solution. Part of it is the genuine enjoyment of imparting knowledge.

Every hour you help a subordinate to master a new task, every moment you spare to share your experience with new recruits, every word of encouragement you give, will fortify your position. When you have a following of people who regard your input as having been instrumental to their personal development, then you will know you have truly got somewhere. It is also intensely satisfying and rewarding.

What is extraordinary is how many mid-level managers fail to recognise the power such an approach holds. They remain aloof, indifferent, detached.

Business people commonly use the analogy of rock climbing to describe what it takes to succeed in the commercial world. We have to pull ourselves up, to ascend the heights. This is the wrong metaphor. To go up, you are better served by building your foundations. As this foundation rises in seniority it will surely carry you with it. No one forgets a good teacher and few people are arrogant enough to fire a great one. Above all, bettering the lot of people around you holds an intense joy which competing alone simply doesn't provide. Fear dogs us most when we climb alone.

The takeaway

There will be those beneath you who are looking for guidance even if they are not entirely aware they need it. Taking such people under your wing is not weakness. It is strength. You will discover you have a lot to offer less experienced folk and their loyalty will mean far more than the fleeting endorsement of a senior manager. **Train disciples** and you will differentiate yourself with the organisation as a whole.

Jo sighed. Joan Milroy was right of course. It was just not something she had ever thought about before. It was a weird idea. If she looked back at the three years she had spent at the company, what would she want to be remembered for? The sad part about it was that there wouldn't be anybody who would actually remember her at all.

There was no denying that before she had her daughter, her main focus had been her own career advancement. That didn't leave much time for anyone else. Junior account executives in public relations came and went. It was a revolving door. They came to glean some experience and then typically high-tailed it out to a consultancy where there was more glamour and a bigger paycheck. There was no point putting time into them. And now she had a family at home to get back to. Every working hour was precious. At the end of the day she simply never had time to worry about anyone else's career.

Perhaps it would have made a difference. But, she reflected, she felt no real remorse. What did it matter after all whether or not a bunch of junior people remembered her or not? In the larger scheme of things, it would make no difference. Joan Milroy had no real career track. She was a functionary, static. Even if she flogged herself to the bone, in five years time she would still be an administrator. Perhaps that was why she threw her energies into other people. In fact she seemed to have spent more time cultivating the careers of secretaries working for her than she did developing her own position. Sure, she had a loyal following around the company, but it didn't add up to much now that judgement day had arrived. Joan was still probably only on about half her own salary. Whatever anyone said, that was the only index that mattered. At the end of the day it was all about money.

Step 25. Advise the Advisors

We all love to hate consultants. They breeze in, interview a load of people, deliver a report no one outside the boardroom ever sees and then something unpleasant happens. But the fact is that they are part of the landscape. The consulting trade has exploded from fifty thousand professionals in 1980 to five hundred thousand in 2001.

The interaction of most employees and consultants tends to be testy and suspicious. The average consultant is about twenty-eight, can appear arrogant and is eagerly awaiting the next assignment in Tahiti. To the veterans of a firm under analysis it can often feel much as it must have done to the seasoned veterans of The Great War, when the boys fresh from the fields of Eton led them over the top of the trenches of the Somme.

The assumption (often the correct one) is that the only sure output of a consulting review is the elimination of functions and the loss of jobs. All consultants are under pressure to demonstrate value for money. The easiest way to show results is to propose a strategy which involves the cutting of costs. Cost elimination feeds through immediately to the profit line. By contrast most revenue generation strategies take a while to filter through and even then their results are uncertain and hard to attribute to a cause.

A PACT WITH THE BUTCHER

But just at it represents a threat, so the presence of consultants also offers an opportunity. A typical consultancy project lasts nine months. It is a sure bet that for at least seven of those nine months, all the consulting team is doing is catching up with what the firm already knows about itself. As a friend once phrased it, *'They are borrowing the boss's watch to tell him the time.'* In the last two months, the team attempts to edge ahead and add value. This means that to get its job done, the consultancy firm is dependent on the goodwill of the organisation to help it. That is why you will always find consultants very receptive to ideas. They know too well that good ideas can come from unlikely quarters. That means people like you and me.

This is your opportunity to act. Consultants mostly need qualitative information rather than quantitative – the anecdotal insights into what makes the firm tick, how clients make a purchase, why certain machines and processes behave the way they do, why certain products have been supported and others left to wither, who really makes the decisions. That means subjective data. Subjective means it can be influenced. We talked earlier about becoming a knowledge guardian and the role of knowledge bottlenecks (Step 17). The presence of a consulting firm can act like a search beam, putting the spotlight directly on knowledge guardians that have been lost in the shadows of obscurity. That is your chance to step out of the shade, without losing sight of your main aim (see Step 19 – **Keep to the core**).

In identifying yourself as a source of wisdom to the consultant, you have the opportunity to control or influence a promotional device that is hard to rival. All knowledge guardians need promoters, and consultants can act as excellent promoters. Just make sure you get the accreditation in their slide pack when they present their findings to management.

The takeaway

When the consulting circus rolls into town, most people will run away. Step forward. Position yourself as a knowledge bottleneck. Guide them judiciously in return for profile. Ensure they position you on the winning team post the change process. Consultants are like weapons. You want to be on the right side of the muzzle. **Advise the advisors.**

A TALE OF TWO DISMISSALS

'So John, is it true then? He's had consultants in. Why didn't you tell us earlier?' Jo asked angrily.

'Joan saw them as well. Why are you asking me? Ask her.'

'They must be at the root of this. You must know,' Jo continued.

'It sounds like you're accusing me of hiring them,' retorted John.

'Well, you're the one who's close to the CFO. It would seem logical.'

'If you really want to know I never so much as talked to them. As far as I know they spent the whole time in the subsidiaries. That's where all the serious cutbacks are probably going to come from. They always do.'

'You really know nothing then?'

'If you want to know, ask Joan. She's been their point of contact here in London.'

'Joan. Why Joan? Sorry, I don't mean to sound rude, but that sounds bizarre.'

Joan Milroy smiled innocently. 'It's our auditors. They were given a list of people to talk to internally. I just set the meetings up. That's what administrators do. They administrate.'

'Why didn't you mention it earlier?' Jo asked irritably.

'What's there to mention?'

'Didn't they pump you for information?'

'What information could I give them? As John keeps reminding me, I'm no one special.'

'But didn't they ask for names.'

'I really can't remember Jo. Besides I'm not sure

Drinkwater would like to find me telling all and sundry what passes through his office.'

'Drinkwater asked you to do this? Really?'

'Jo, you're making too much of this. As I said I'm an administrator. And that's as far as it goes. John's the manager.' Joan smiled conspiratorially. 'He knows more than I ever will about these things.'

Step 26. Look backwards as well as forwards

If there is one certain thing about the uncertain course of history, it is that the historians go down in history. For in writing history, they have the chance to rewrite it. Only emperors and dictators are afforded the same opportunity.

Almost every aspect of the history of humanity has been documented. From crusaders to cave dwellers, from saints to peasants, from Nepal to Notting Hill – somewhere a history will have been written. But there is one great gaping hole in the historical map – companies. Forty per cent of Western humanity is employed in some sort of company. Most of us spend fifty per cent of our lives harnessed to these institutions. They pay our mortgages, educate our children and put food on the table. Yet virtually none have histories written about them.

All firms are anxious about their longevity and all CEOs are anxious about their posterity. It is one of the pressing facts of corporate life that few firms live beyond forty years – the average individual career span. That means the history of firms is little more than the biography of a human life. If approached by someone like Simon Schama few of us would refuse to have our biographies written. The same is true of companies. All firms want to think they will last forever, all are hungry for history.

But the reason so few firms have any history is that there is typically no one around long enough to compile it. Up until the early eighties there was great credibility associated with having been loyal and long-serving. Firms tended to do things the way they always had and valued continuity. The only route to the top was a long internal apprenticeship. Venerability was honoured. Things have since changed out of all recognition. It is hard to find anyone who has spent more than twenty years in most firms.

Some firms do of course buck the trend. Many of the big, blue chip corporates with household brands tend to have a keen sense of their heritage and history. And that is partly why they have endured the test of years when most have fallen around them. The senior management process in such firms is as much about reputation preservation as it is about making money.

You may be no Schama, but you will be as well-positioned as anyone to unearth the history of the firm you work in – how it was founded, what events shaped it, how its strategy has evolved, and what makes it unique. Mastery of these facts will put you in a strong position. You will be able to put everything in context. You will be deferred to as an historian. If you understand the evolution of the firm, you will find yourself the point of reference for all sorts of enquiries. You will be attributed with knowledge and wisdom on which you have no real claim. That's fine. If you are the one historian in a firm you can rewrite history to suit you. That is what historians do. It means being informed, speaking with authority about the provenance of the firm and articulating its values.

The takeaway

Pulling together the history of the firm, particularly its founding values, will take a few weeks, but not months. Once you have the bedrock in place you can always add to it. Once you are in control of this material, you will discover your reputation as a historian will grow. You will be asked to contribute to the website, to write for the company newsletter. You will be a point of continuity in a troubled world of change. That is a great thing to be. **Look backwards as well as forwards.**

A TALE OF TWO DISMISSALS

'So Joan', John Mowbray continued in his vaguely condescending tone, 'you've been here the longest. Is Jo right? Has all this happened before?'

'You mean have people been laid off? Of course they have. You tell me. Isn't that what business is like?'

'What I mean is, is this something Drinkwater's known for doing?'

'You know how he started the company, don't you?'

'Of course.'

'Then you know what he's done in the past. Ask yourself what that tells you about him.'

John Mowbray was silent for a while.

'Well maybe I've forgotten. Tell me,' he added somewhat sheepishly after a pause.

Joan shrugged her shoulders. 'You know. It amazes me. You join a company and you don't even bother to find out anything about its past.'

'Come on Joan. This is all about the future. The past is past.'

'If you want to know the future look to the past and you'll find it. History always repeats itself. That's one of the many benefits of getting older.'

'So, in your crystal ball does the company crash?'

'It's obvious you know nothing about John Drinkwater. He doesn't let things fail. Anyone who knows him knows that. If you don't know it, you're going to find out.'

Step 27. Move the goalposts

Employment is a sort of game. We learn the rules, spend most of our career dribbling the ball and then, if we are lucky, we have one or two chances to put the ball in the back of the net. Like all games, employment is competitive – the goals are counted. The scoring takes the form of the annual performance review. We all are subject to them. Once a year, just like everyone else, you will be evaluated on aptitude and delivery.

Performance evaluation is often given the gloss of being there for the benefit of us the employee – like a school exam in Maths. It feels awful now but when we are grown up we will look back with gratitude. But in reality the evaluation process is a control mechanism. It is there to ensure we are properly tuned, and performing to spec. Implicitly it assumes we can all be treated the same and our performance evaluated along uniform lines. Often we are left with the nagging sense that it in no way captures our contribution to the company.

At its core, the annual performance review is a low cost exercise. It is also one way. The bosses evaluate the bossed. And when it comes to redundancy time, evaluation rankings can become the tools of our destruction.

Hopefully, everything we have gone through about achieving differentiation will tell you to beware of uniformity. If you are judged on the same basis as everyone else you are doomed to a low-cost position.

It is usually impossible to opt out of a performance evaluation system employed firm-wide. But what you can do is actively introduce a complementary set of criteria against which your contribution can be judged. The easiest and most advantageous set of alternatives will have emerged from your list of value drivers. You now know where you add most value to your employer and the precise impact your involvement has on the success of the firm. If you clearly communicate where you are delivering value, and what effect this has on aspects of firm performance, you will be able to influence how you are assessed. Few of us are usually this enterprising in our approach to evaluation. But as evaluation methods become more qualitative and consultative, the leeway to influence the criteria will probably increase.

The takeaway

Your list of value drivers will be most effective if you get yourself judged against those criteria. **Move the goalposts** and in the process you will differentiate yourself. It is always easier to score if you kick from the penalty spot and the keeper is on your side.

A TALE OF TWO DISMISSALS

John Mowbray was only in there for perhaps a couple of minutes, but to Jo it felt like a lifetime. Joan Milroy said nothing. Then almost silently the door swung open and John walked out, looking straight ahead. He didn't even glance at her. But she saw enough of him to known what it meant. Two seconds later he had disappeared through the door back into the fifth floor of the main office. It was the last she was to see of John Mowbray for almost four months.

Thirty seconds later the door to Drinkwater's office opened, and a woman beckoned Jo through. She could feel her heart begin to race, and a knot form so tight in her stomach that she completely forgot what is was she had determined to say. The room was large, with a high ceiling and four vast windows with a panorama over the Thames. Jo had expected to see a couple of people with Drinkwater, but to her surprise there were six people seated around the conference table. There were stacks of paper scattered across the surface, and a look of fatigue on the six faces staring at her.

She scanned them all, her mind racing to take it in. 'Slow down Jo. Calm down. Don't let them see what you're feeling', she kept telling herself. But now the initial surge of panic had been replaced by torpid resignation. Drinkwater wasn't even there. She suddenly felt utterly humiliated. A man at the far end of the table stood up, smiled at her and indicated for her to take the vacant chair. She vaguely recognised a couple of the faces round the table, poring over sheets of paper. But not the man who had addressed her.

'I'm sure you're wondering why you've been asked here? You're probably wondering who we are?'

'Well, yes, I am,' Jo responded tonelessly.

'We represent the consulting firm which has been appointed by the board of Communicopia to review its cost position in light of recent performance . . .'

Jo didn't need to hear more. It was what she thought. It was like being interviewed by your executioners. She only half heard the words being spoken to her. The room seemed to be drifting vaguely in and out of focus.

'. . . it is not a decision the company has undertaken lightly. I am afraid after much deliberation, it has been concluded that the needs of the business and the skills you can offer are no longer a good match . . .'

Jo watched his lips move, and the frown lines on his forehead. It was surreal, like watching a time-lapse sequence of some distant film. The words seemed disembodied, insubstantial.

'Are no longer a match . . .' she repeated to herself. Whenever had anything at Communicopia been a match? The idea was ludicrous. Then they came; the words she had thought she would never hear.

'You are to be made redundant commencing immediately. In the interests of security, you will be accompanied to your desk to clear your personal effects and then the board expects you to leave in good faith . . .'

'In good faith . . .' Jo repeated to herself. What faith? What was he talking about?

'. . . in reflection of your past services to the company, the board has decided to extend the statutory terms of your employment contract. You will be given three months severance, including pension contribution, and private medical cover . . .'

In retrospect, Jo reflected what a callous affair the whole encounter had been. She had been so taken aback by the shock that she hadn't even questioned the terms they had offered her. It was too late now. The ploy had worked. She had signed the document and it was done. It was not until later that afternoon, as she sat on the train back to West Byfleet, that she realised what a mistake she had made. The grey suburbs slid by with utter dreariness. God knows what she had done.

It was not until almost a year later that Jo Parker and John Mowbray bumped into each other again. It was a complete fluke. They had never interacted socially, and they lived in very different worlds. She had agonised about whether to take the case to tribunal but, in the end, had decided she couldn't face the anxiety and stress involved. She had learnt from friends that three months pay was more than many of their contemporaries were getting. Besides she had Joanne to take care of, and three months together was what she felt she needed right now.

But by February the bank account had slipped quietly into overdraft and she knew she would have to look for another job, however painful it would be. The firing had knocked her confidence badly. She never thought it could happen to her. They had given her a reference. But any future employer was going to see exactly what had happened. She was marked with failure. It would probably mean she would have to take a major demotion to get back in the workforce.

She hadn't given John Mowbray a thought since that fateful day waiting in Drinkwater's miserable office. As she cleared her desk she had heard that, as she thought, he too had been given the push. It had really surprised her that he was deemed unnecessary. It did something to draw the sting from her own sense of inadequacy. But after that she had put him entirely out of her mind. Then, eleven months later, here they were again, waiting together to be interviewed. It was extraordinary.

John seemed changed. He looked older than his thirty-one years, and the arrogant curl to his smile had gone. It had probably been harder for him. At least she had a family to look after. He recognised her immediately, and despite the awkwardness of the situation, seemed genuinely glad to see her again. The conversation quickly got back to Communicopia.

'Yes, Joan Milroy was the one they decided to keep.'

'It seems utterly bizarre,' Jo said vitriolically. 'She was only a petty administrator. And she was old. What can she possibly have had that we didn't. I always suspected that company was stupid. But that just about confirms it for sure.'

'Didn't you know then?' John Mowbray continued in a subdued tone.

'Know what?'

'She was the one who apparently put the list together.'

'What list?'

'The list of people the company could live without.'

'Joan? What are you talking about, John?'

'The consultants. You remember.'

'Of course, but what of it?'

'They apparently used the administrators to give them names. They had no idea who they could purge without destroying the business. Turns out they were probably right. We underestimated the likes of Joan Milroy. Haven't you seen the share price? It's back up at six pounds per share.'

'Six pounds? No I hadn't noticed. That means all those options would have been worth something after all.'

'Too right. But also too late now.'

Jo stared ahead in silence hardly able to believe what she had just heard.

'I've been thinking about the whole thing,' John Mowbray continued. 'You and I, we both made a mistake you know. We should have listened to Joan. I think she was trying to tell us something during that time we spent waiting for Drinkwater. But I don't think either of us were prepared to listen.'

'There was nothing I could learn from her. She wasn't even qualified.'

'If I didn't know better, I'd think that sounded like arrogance, Jo. I don't know about you, but I've learnt something through all this.'

Jo shrugged her shoulders. What did she have to lose after all? She listened to John in subdued silence.

Step 28. Think three years

Most of the decision-making in firms is intensely short-term. The people at the top of organisations typically think in three year chunks. The reason is a pretty good one. This is their average life expectancy. Moreover, option plans of the size necessary to lure top-dogs to the board usually mature over a short period of time. They are invariably triggered by appreciation in share price – precisely the same motive driving institutional investors in the company. That means all the powers that be are geared to driving results in the short-term and, more specifically, to pushing up the share price. Around three years would be typical.

This can wreak havoc amongst normal employees. Most of us are emotionally geared to much longer time frames. Top executives may express their determination to change things but we instinctively cling to continuity. Continuity is a fundamental social need we all share, and routine is very important to maintaining a sense of well being. Continuity of salary means we can risk the egregious mortgage, the car payments, the school fees. As employees we mostly think five to ten years. The predictability of the work routine underpins our lives.

So employer and employee diverge quite dramatically, one moving at eighty miles-an-hour and switching lanes, the other at fifty and sticking to the slow lane of the highway of life. It is this critical difference in motive and timeframe that pits management against the grain of the organisation. That is also why there is so often a phenomenal amount of disruption as management battles to impose the change necessary to deliver short-term results.

The reality is most social structures have more continuity and stability than people give them credit for. Patterns of behaviour and interaction are hard to break. That is why corporate change programmes often fail. The social inertia in most firms is enormous. This does not sit well with contemporary management expectations. The fall-out from the collision of boss and bossed is a trail of redundancy.

BE A ROLLING STONE, NOT A STATIC ROCK

We have explored more than two dozen tricks to beating the odds of getting fired, but you should not make the mistake of thinking this is a long-term strategy. There is no such thing as long-term in employment. If you have a mental model that presupposes a minimum of ten years employment and a pension, that may not be compatible with contemporary reality. Far better to calibrate yourself to the same timescale as the CEO. Your personal strategic plan should have a three year span. That means you have a clear timeframe in which to show you can add some value. You also have a similar window in which to maximise your learning about the industry in which you work, to inculcate loyal subordinates, to communicate your value effectively, to master the idiosyncrasies of share price and the language of finance – in short, to master the critical steps to commercial longevity and, above all, to prove to yourself that you can achieve a position of differentiation. If you can become firmly differentiated, the life of work will be a far more joyful, stress-free event. That means both you and it will last longer.

The takeaway

The clock is ticking. No time to idle around reading books. Get a move on!

Select Bibliography

The world is awash with books, and our lives are so short of time, but here is a selection of books containing ideas you might find enlightening in your quest for differentiation:

Fish!: A remarkable way to boost morale and improve results, Lundin, S.C., Paul, H. & Christensen, J, Hodder Mobius, London, 2001.

Heartland, Scott, M.C., John Wiley and Sons Ltd, London, 2001.

Reinspiring the Corporation, Scott, M.C., John Wiley and Sons Ltd, London, 2001.

The Elephant and the Flea, Handy, C., Hutchinson, London, 2001.

The Empty Raincoat, Handy, C., Random House Business Books, London, 1995.

The Hungry Spirit, Handy, C., Random House Business Books, London, 1998.

The Okinawa Way, Willcox, B., Willcox, C., & Suzuki, M., Penguin, London, 2001.

The Road Less Travelled, Peck, M.S., Arrow, London, 1990.

The Seven Habits of Highly Successful People, Covey, S.R., Simon & Schuster, US, 1990.

Who Moved My Cheese? Johnson, Dr S., Vermillion, London, 1999.

OTHER TITLES AVAILABLE FROM RANDOM HOUSE BUSINESS BOOKS

A GOOD HARD KICK IN THE ASS

Rob Adams

The concept of a 'new economy' spawned a dangerous misconception: that a fundamentally new and different approach to business was required. *A Good Hard Kick in the Ass* debunks each myth chapter-by-chapter, providing realism rather than hype.

Rob Adams is the founder of AV Labs, an investment and strategy fund with backing of $60 million. At Lotus he helped drive revenues past a billion dollars before the company was bought by IBM. He interviewed 40–50 entrepreneurs, executives and founders of established businesses, marketing and strategic research gurus and academics as part of his research for *A Good Hard Kick in the Ass*.

Good Girl's Guide to Negotiating

How to negotiate effectively without being a bitch

Leslie Whitaker and Elizabeth Austin

'*The Good Girl's Guide to Negotiating* has chapters on everything from pre-nups to divorce settlements, and has simple instructions for dealing with doctors, lawyers and bosses . . . 'Negotiating with liars', 'getting out of an ambush' and 'creating a diversion' are just some of the lessons for more advanced students. ****' *Woman's Way*

'Forget your good girl image – go in and haggle for that pay rise.' *Evening Standard*

'This female-friendly guide to everyday bargaining skills and strategies is essential for those seeking career success and personal fulfilment . . . To sharpen your negotiating skills, this indispensable book, with step-by-step tips and positive case studies, may be the answer.' *ABTA Business Travel Magazine*

Everyone needs to know how to negotiate effectively. *The Good Girl's Guide to Negotiating* emphasises how women can play to their strengths – listening astutely, interpreting body language, empathy and relationship building – and how they can overcome their weaknesses.

Contents:

Good Girls: why it's hard for women to negotiate a fair deal

Getting to You: understanding what you want is the first win in win-win negotiating

Girl Power: listening and empathizing are key skills in negotiating

Prep time: research and rehearsal

Table manners: why small talk can make a difference, seating arrangements and talking tough

The Negotiation Dance: searching for a breakthrough solution with your opponent

Countering Common Boy Ploys: how to handle negotiating tricks

It Ain't Over Until It's Over: tips for concluding every deal successfully

Execution

The Discipline of Getting Things Done

Larry Bossidy and Ram Charan with Charles Burck

'A great practitioner and an insightful theorist join forces to write a compelling business story of "how to get it done".' *Jack Welch*

The Book That Shows *How* to Get the Job Done and Deliver Results . . . whether you're running an entire company or in your first management job

'Good practical insight and advice on managing for results at firms of any size. Execution is key and this book clearly explains what it means and how it brings together the critical elements of any organization – its people, strategies, and operations.' *L.R. Raymond, Chairman and CEO, Exxon Mobil*

'The best thought-out plans in the world aren't worth the paper they're written on if you can't pull them off. And that's what this book is all about. *Execution: The Discipline of Getting Things Done* is well written and gives sound, practical advice about how to make things happen. It is well worth the reading.' *Ralph S. Larsen, Chairman and CEO, Johnson & Johnson*

'For those managers who have struggled to make it happen, fix a problem, get it done – or otherwise transform winning strategies into genuine results — here's the missing medicine from two who know from long experience what works and what doesn't. Larry Bossidy and Ram Charan offer a compelling leadership prescription, and it comes down to realism, discipline, and above all, great execution.' *Michael Useem, Professor of Management and Director of the Center for Leadership and Change, Wharton School, University of Pennsylvania*

The Elephant and the Flea

Charles Handy

Charles Handy's bestselling new book looks at how individuals (the fleas in his analogy) relate to multi-national conglomerates (the elephants). In addition to addressing how and why we work today, he covers a wide range of preoccupations and issues including the increasing fear of big business.

'*The Elephant and the Flea* is disarmingly honest ... the book should be widely read for its candour, good sense and mature practical wisdom.' *Times Literary Supplement*

'Intensely personal yet remarkably universal, the book is another provocative, illuminating, and enjoyable work from the oil executive turned bestselling author.' *Amazon.com editor review*

'Handy's style is personal, anecdotal and entirely jargon-free. His reference points are diverse and unexpected. He puzzles about problems we can all recognize.' *Financial Times*

'This latest offering is a joy to read. It is one of those rare things, a book by a management author that you want to devour at one sitting.' *Ambassador*

'Its eclectic style makes it extremely enjoyable.' *The Irish Times*

'He has that rare gift among business writers – able to talk sense and leave out the jargon ... This title will appeal to a very wide audience, because it is everything a business book should be – very readable and thought-provoking.' *Business and Computer Bookseller*

Charles Handy is a writer and broadcaster, whose books have sold over one million copies around the world.

BOO HOO

$135 million, 18 months and 400 people . . .

Ernst Malmsten, Erik Portanger and Charles Drazin

'enthralling' *The Financial Times*

'Such a dazzling version of the boo phenomenon that as readers turn the pages they will be rooting for the company to survive even though they know the story ends in disaster.' *The Sunday Times*

'*boo hoo* is an engrossing account of how two childhood friends persuaded some of the world's savviest investors and fashion houses – including Bernard Arnault's LVMH and the Benetton family – to fund a sports and designer clothing company to the tune of $100m.' *The Guardian*

'The game would be to bring boo.com to market, when it would soon be worth more than $1 billion and make its backers rich. Can all this have happened last year? It seems more like a tale from a different aeon, but the lessons it teaches are timeless.' *The Spectator*

'One of the hottest books on the shelves at Waterstones.' *Sunday Times Style Magazine*

'*boo hoo* . . . is 386 pages of oddly gripping text made nearly unbelievable by the amount of money that was given voluntarily to two twentysomething Swedes . . . the very readable book . . . adds lurid colour to [the] story.' *The Daily Telegraph*

'Reading [this] has the fascination of watching a high-speed car crash replayed in slow motion. You know what's going to happen, you can see the confident glow on the drivers' faces, but can't warn them about the curve in the road that is coming to unstick them. *Schadenfreude* is irresistible. And yet everyone walks away unhurt.' *The Independent*

The Next Big Idea

The big ideas for business in the 21st century

Carol Kennedy

'Written with a freshness and sparkle that belie a considerable amount of research, and provides new insights on almost every page.' *Innovation Magazine*

'Carol Kennedy's *The Next Big Idea* should be on the desk of every consultant.' *Accountancy Age*

Management in the 20th century was perpetually driven by the hunt for the Big Idea – the breakthrough that would bring greater efficiency, performance, productivity and profits to the business organisation and greater motivation to its employees.

This book investigates where business will take its new big ideas from, whether from new kinds of gurus, research institutes studying the lessons of natural science, practical industrialists working out problems on the factory floor, or the best brains of Silicon Valley.

Carol Kennedy is an award-winning business and management writer and author of the best-selling *Guide to the Management Gurus* (new edition 2002), which has been translated into over a dozen languages, and its companion book *Managing With the Gurus*.